Astrology Beyond Ego

QUEST BOOKS
are published by
The Theosophical Society in America,
a branch of a world organization
dedicated to the promotion of brotherhood and
the encouragement of the study of religion,
philosophy, and science, to the end that man may
better understand himself and his place in
the universe. The Society stands for complete
freedom of individual search and belief.
In the Theosophical Classics Series
well-known occult works are made
available in popular editions.

Cover art by *Jane A. Evans*

Astrology Beyond Ego

TIM LYONS

This publication made possible with
the assistance of the Kern Foundation

The Theosophical Publishing House
Wheaton, Ill. U.S.A.
Madras, India / London, England

The Theosophical Publishing House
306 West Geneva Road
Wheaton, IL 60187

A publication of the Theosophical Publishing House, a department
of the Theosophical Society in America.

Library of Congress Cataloging in Publication Data

Lyons, Tim, 1949-
  Astrology beyond ego.

  "A Quest original"—T.p. verso.
  Bibliography: p.
  Includes index.
  1. Astrology. I. Title.
BF1708.1.L96   1986   133.5   86-40123
ISBN 0-8356-0612-0 (pbk.)

Printed in the United States of America

Contents

Acknowledgments

Astrology is an ancient practice, based on knowledge which has been passed down through the centuries. Any astrologer is therefore deeply indebted to those who have gone before. In the twentieth century, astrological practice has undergone dramatic and profound changes as it has incorporated knowledge from analytical psychology, sociology, history, and even computer science. Because of this, the modern astrologer's most obvious indebtedness is to his contemporaries or near contemporaries, those who have reinterpreted astrological tradition into a modern idiom.

Foremost among these, both generally and for this work in particular, is Dane Rudhyar, whose many works have pioneered a trail in humanistic and transpersonal astrology which have set a tone for contemporary astrology that is hard to gauge. I would also like to acknowledge an indebtedness to some writers whose influence on this book goes beyond what can be indicated through footnotes: Stephen Arroyo, for his ability to see both the enlightened and the neurotic side of astrological indications; Robert Hand, for explications of the symbols which incorporate both ancient knowledge and modern needs; Liz Greene, particularly for her work with projection and with the outer planets; and Alan Oken, particularly for his work with the historical manifestation of astrological symbols. In the sections on Chiron, I am indebted to Erminie Lantero's work, which remains the primary source for material on the recently discovered planetoid.

Less directly influential but no less significant was the instruction received in Taoist movement arts from Paul B. Gallagher, and in the Western acting tradition from Linda Putnam. I am also thankful to the Lakota people of Pine

Ridge, South Dakota, for opening my eyes to magic of the world. The many writings of Frank Waters have also been important in this respect.

Shirley Nicholson of Quest Books and Robert Donath did very important work in refining the manuscript and helping to bring it into its final form. Without their aid, this book would have been much less coherent. An able and sensitive editor is an enormous gift to any writer, and I am most grateful to them for their work and kindness.

Finally, I would like to acknowledge my indebtedness to my root guru, Vidyadhara the Venerable Chogyam Trungpa, Rinpoche, and to the Kagyu Lineage of Tibetan Buddhism, from whom I have been fortunate enough to receive teachings.

1

Astrology and Perennial Wisdom

There is a joke you may have heard about three men who find themselves on a desert island. They are sitting there wondering how to get back home when they discover a lamp. Naturally they rub the lamp, and just as naturally a genie emerges and grants each man a wish. The first man, who is French, wishes to be back in Paris and is immediately whisked away. The second man, who is English, wishes to be back in London and is instantly transported there. The third man, who is of whatever nationality at whose expense the joke is being made, ponders a moment and innocently says, "Gee, I liked those two guys. I wish they were back here!"

The traditional interpretation of the joke, if jokes have traditional interpretations, is that the third man lacked the vision of his two fellows. He couldn't see beyond the limits of his present situation (though he seemed to put a higher value on human fellowship than the others!). The first two men at least had some common sense and some notion of where they wanted to be instead of where they were, a notion considered to be of some value in our age of constant mobility.

Another interpretation might be, however, that all three men were somewhat foolish, because all three wished for something directly in line with their habitual patterns. All three responses display a lack of imagination on that level; and none of the men is able to see beyond the limits of his desires. A person of vision might have seen the island as a splendid place for meditative retreat and wished only for an enlightened person to come and teach him the preliminary techniques for spiritual development.

There is a parallel in this joke to our customary use of astrological knowledge. The knowledge is like a genie, not in that it will grant us any wish we might have, but in that it puts our personal situation into a different perspective and provides us with some apparent power. Like the men in the joke, we can put this power of perspective in service either to our habitual patterns and reference points, or to some commitment to grow beyond those limits. Astrology can aid us by putting habitual patterns and reference points into objective focus, and it can provide us with alternatives that are in harmony with our basic nature. However, it is up to us how we use this knowledge and perspective.

In other words, astrological knowledge can provide either the ego-serving power that comes from mere information; or that other sort of power, which we can call "transformative," which is an element of wisdom.

In general, contemporary astrological practice centers on the interpretation of individual horoscopes. The astrological symbol system is applied toward the elucidation of an individual's character or destiny, usually with reference to the person's own hopes, fears, and desires. The goal seems to be to assist a person in finding greater meaning, relevance, usefulness, understanding, or empowerment in his or her* life. Hidden potentials may be revealed, and blockages may be brought forth to give the person a sense of process and growth.

These practices have obvious value, and it is not at all my purpose to denigrate them. Anything that can ease suffering and give a sense of meaning would seem to be laudatory. In providing this helpful perspective, however, the astrologer

---

*The masculine pronouns (he, his, him) will be used from time to time for ease of expression only and should be understood to include women as well as men.

should also have perspective on the activity itself. Very often, astrological information serves primarily to reinforce a person's self-concept. This may not seem to be a problem at first, especially as there *are* many people whose shaky self-concept leads to suffering. It seems important to give them some support and objectivity on just what their "self" consists of and just what its inner potentials might be.

Still, we must be careful of what we do. First of all, we must realize that even with the severely troubled, there are many harmful forms of self-fixation that perpetuate suffering rather than heal it. Unfortunately, astrology can aid this sort of fixation by providing it with a conceptual, even purportedly "cosmic" foundation. It is well to remember that according to Buddhist teachings—and, somewhat less specifically, other systems of spiritual work—fixation is a *cause* of suffering, not a solution. This includes fixation on "I" or "me"and "my problems."

One of the assumptions presented herein is that if we are to present astrology properly and fully, our presentation must be consistent with the logic of the system itself. Great harm can result when systems of spiritual knowledge or human development are presented in ego-serving ways. The history of many of the world's major religions amply demonstrates this, and though astrologers are not likely to organize themselves into any sort of political or military force (as so often happens with religions), we should be just as cognizant of presenting our teachings in their pure form. Knowledge does not now, nor has it ever, implied its own most enlightened usage.

The purpose of this book is to explore this "pure form" of astrology through examining the inner logic of the symbol systems which compose it, and then to explore some of the implications and corollaries of that inner logic as it applies to relationship, freedom, the current socio-political situation, and spiritual growth.

Our situation using astrology is somewhat like our relationship to the earth itself. The earth has its various cycles, symbols, materials, and wonders. In this modern age, we often

think first of how we can "use" these for our supposed betterment. This concern for usage becomes harmful if it blinds us
to the true nature of what we use. Our use of things is often
intimately, and at first sight inextricably, interwoven with our
ego-driven desires. As we shall see, astrological symbolism
demonstrates that ego is, first, not a solid thing on which to
base wise decisions, and second, a confusion which needs to
be transformed.

We develop a true and fruitful relationship to the earth by
being in harmony with the earth itself, by understanding its
own inner workings. The same may be said for an astrologer's
relationship to the astrological system of knowledge. Both the
earth and astrology contain meaning in themselves, and to
understand that meaning we need to observe them as they
are, in their own nature, without specific reference to application. Only then can we use them in a harmonious and ultimately fruitful way.

Our use of astrology, then, must be in harmony with the
nature of the system itself. We will find that, like the earth,
this system has its own inner order, its own inner logic. This
order and logic is evident first of all in the meaning, or even
the teaching, that arises from the ordering of the planets, signs,
and houses. The discovery of this inner order may then be extended to the use of various traditional astrological practices
such as transits, progressions, rulerships, mundane astrology,
and so forth. There is a meaning in these practices even before they are applied to individual cases. The meaning is in
the logic of the usage itself.

The same may be said for the *I Ching*, the Chinese *Book
of Changes*. Like the astrological symbol system, the sixty-
four-hexagram system of the *I Ching* may be used either as
a system of divination or as a book of wisdom (a systematic
statement of knowledge leading to and revealing underlying
wisdom). The sixty-four hexagrams have their own internal
order, which may be viewed from various perspectives, and
they present an ordered and fairly precise view of the world
in which we live. (This "view" is contained in the text itself
and in the traditional Commentaries written on that basic
text, commentaries which are generally presented as append-

ages, or "Wings" to the text itself.) Although one might use the *I Ching* as a book of simple divination, its most proper and complete use includes a knowledge of and respect for the world view which the book implies, embodies, and grows from.

Astrology, like the *I Ching*, is an organized group of symbols which have demonstrated relevance to the human condition. Also like the *I Ching*, astrological symbols may be used for either divination or wisdom. In the case of astrology, however, there are some major differences. First, we are without traditional commentaries of unquestioned relevance. Second, the astrological system does not come from a single cultural tradition (whereas the *I Ching*, for example, is obviously Chinese, though it mixes Taoist and Confucian elements). For this reason, the philosophical foundation or basis of astrology is more difficult to trace. Any definitive statement about these foundations, which we may call the "roots" of the astrological tree, will best come from the fruits, by which we will "know" the system if we eat thoughtfully enough.

The modern astrologer is one eater of this fruit. The fact that the fruit is still healthy indicates that the root is still intact, and that the roots are still connected to the trunk and branches of the tree. Astrology is still in touch with its hidden origins. But we must eat thoughtfully if we are to have a full feeling for the tree and for the life-giving qualities of the fruit. (It may also be a good idea to check the fruit for worms, especially the worm of ego, which so readily invades even the healthiest trees.)

In this book, an attempt is made to look more closely at the basic, structural implications of astrology, at its foundations or philosophic base, by examining the fruit of the astrological tree, fruit which has proven itself healthy through actual life-giving application. But more particularly, this volume examines the inner core of the fruit—the pit, or pith, or seeds—for the core is a microcosm of the tree itself, containing all its potentials.

Looking at this core means that I am not dealing so much with the pulp of the fruit, the life-giving juices of individual application. This area is well covered by other astrological writers. In dealing with this dark, inner area of the fruit, I may at times seem to be a bit obdurate, taking a "hard line" or dark point of view. I think this results from the attempt to integrate astrological implications with the demands of spiritual work, because there is a "hard line" quality to much spiritual work. But one may look at the paintings of old Taoist recluses and see that this hard line leads to, and even contains, abundant joy.

On another level, this work attempts to address the larger question: What does astrology imply about the human condition? Astrological symbology is discussed from the standpoint of its inherent, perennial wisdom. This wisdom is not lacking in practical value, but this value cannot be appropriated by ego. In the end, the perennial wisdom of astrology is that it directs us, through the inner logic of its symbols, to see the necessity of spiritual growth for human beings. The sum and substance of the hard line is that the solidity of ego is an illusion, an illusion which always tries to appropriate everything for itself, but which is in the end only a limitation that obscures our vision, our freedom, and our ability to relate fully with others.

Most astrologers would probably agree that their work deals with and gives symbolic form to some fundamental truths and energies that work through human existence and experience. Astrological symbols both reveal and embody basic truths. The distinctive goal of this book is to show how these truths emerge not only from any symbol taken in isolation, but in how they work together as a whole system. Just as the individual hexagrams of the *I Ching* have meaning in themselves, yet take on wider and deeper implications when considered in relation to the entirety of the system, so in astrology the individual symbols (planets, signs, and houses) have individual meanings which become even more significant when seen in the context of the entire interwoven system.

This is not a completely unprecedented approach. Dane Rudhyar's work often addresses the astrological symbols in a similar way. The difference is that I have focused on specific human issues, asking specific questions to see what response comes from the astrological tradition

The second chapter forms a basis for those that follow. It examines ego from an astrological perspective. More specifically, it asks: Does the astrological symbol system agree with many other spiritual traditions in which ego, or fixated self-concept, is a limiting factor and an illusion which one must overcome and see through? I shall answer this by emphasizing the processes of organic and psychological development implied by the planets, signs, and houses. I will attempt to see if these implications can be connected to the process of ego and self-fixation, and then to those processes and energies that allow one to see through ego's game and go beyond it.

My conclusion is that astrological symbols *do* direct us beyond our ego-fixation. This does not necessarily mean that an astrologer should insist that a client direct all his or her energies toward self-transcendence. First of all, a client may not be at a stage in life where such a "transpersonal process" (to use Rudhyar's term) will make sense or take root. Secondly, the astrologer himself or herself may not be involved in the transpersonal process (at least not consciously), and so would not—and perhaps should not—counsel it to others.

There is a parallel here, between the practice of the astrological counsellor and the vocation of a priest. Not all priests are mystics, and much of a priest's ministry deals with problems much more mundane than spiritual *angst*. Parishioners are likely to come to the priest with marriage problems, difficulties with an alcoholic relative, or any one of a multitude of difficulties that do not seem directly related to the well-being of their soul. Still, the priest has presumably studied theology, the basis of the religious belief on which he bases his counsel. He realizes that he owes these beliefs a deep allegiance and that they must in some way permeate his work with people, even if they do not appear on the surface.

The priest will also realize that people come to him at different stages of their spiritual journey. Not everyone is at a major turning-point of spiritual growth. Still, the priest should be able to recognize a true spiritual crisis when he sees one. He will recognize that such a crisis is integral to his own faith, and that it is at the basis of any belief and true growth into the knowledge which that faith preaches. It is, in the end, to that knowledge that he owes allegiance; and if he cannot, in his own person, give spiritual guidance based on the roots of that knowledge, he must be ready to send a person to someone who is able to work at that level.

Similarly, the astrologer is usually confronted with problems and questions which do not, on the surface, seem to embody a spiritual crisis (though of course one must always look beneath the surface: what appears as merely mundane may embody something much more profound). The astrologer needs, first, to recognize the dignity of all questions and difficulties brought before him, which means to recognize the dignity of human suffering. Beyond that, the astrologer needs to be like the priest in his allegiance to the truths of his faith, and he will recognize that the alleviation of suffering will come through an application of these truths. In order to see these truths, he must examine the symbols through which they are presented.

In the end, the astrologer is like any counselor in that he needs to work from and with compassion, uniting that compassion with vision. The astrologer has one advantage over priests and other counselors, however. The astrological symbols upon which he bases his counsel have obvious connections to both mundane and spiritual experience. Thus the astrologer is able to see the spiritual process embodied and embedded in apparently mundane events and difficulties. The priest may also intuit this connection, but it is not usually so precisely worked out through the symbols of his faith. Also, like the priest, when confronted with a spiritual crisis beyond his depth of experience, the astrologer should recognize his own limitations and be willing to refer a client to another practitioner more able to deal with a certain situation. The ability to counsel businesses does not imply the ability to counsel on the spiritual path (and vice versa). As Jung pointed out, one cannot counsel others at a level beyond that which one has reached oneself.

The fifth chapter examines the relationship between the transformative and collective applications of the outer planets.

These planets, the "trans-Saturnian" or transcendental planets, symbolize on the one hand, the stages and energies involved in the transformation of ego, and on the other collective trends in thinking, feeling, and public consciousness. This chapter touches on an essential issue in our modern world: the relationship between our need for spiritual growth and the tremendous problems we see on all sides in collective life.

The sixth and seventh chapters examine human relationships and intimacy. Here the question is simply: What does the astrological symbol system teach us about present-day crises in relationships? The approach in these chapters is more eclectic. Though the basis of the discussion is always astrological, the path leads through mythology, history, and ecology. Though the conclusion may be again that problems in relationships result from ego-clinging, the perspective is somewhat different, given in a more particularized context.

The eighth chapter deals with the issue of freedom. Some astrological transits are examined, and the question raised is: What does this practice—and astrology generally—imply about human freedom? The answer is, of course, not a simple one, not simply that freedom does or does not exist. First, one must decide what is meant by freedom. Second, one must see that our notions of freedom are generally intertwined with our notions about ego. It is generally "I"—or some sense of solidity—that wants to be free. The logic in this book leads to a notion of freedom somewhat different from the one we normally use. This new freedom is at once more demanding and more freeing, somewhat like Jesus' "narrow gate" or the demands of the Hinayana (small vehicle) stage of Buddhist practice.

This book is not intended only for students of astrology but for anyone interested in the path beyond ego. Therefore, astrological terminology is defined in the glossary.

Finally, I should point out that although numerous references are made in this book to spiritual teachings (particularly Buddhist), no claim is made that they stand as complete or traditional interpretations of these teachings. Anyone who wishes to investigate the inner substance or practice of any of these teachings should do so through an authorized spokesperson. If readers realize that the path of the astrologer demands a truly spiritual commitment, and that this commitment involves more than just a conceptual understanding of symbols, then this book may be considered successful. In the end, the major implication of astrological symbolism is that spiritual growth—the growth beyond the blindness of ego—is each person's birthright.

We should always keep in mind that the nature of astrology is conceptual. It is a system of symbols that state and imply a good deal about the human condition, including the need for a spiritual perspective on our lives. By awakening the intellect, astrology can set one on the spiritual path, but astrology is not itself the path. Like a mandala (or should I say other mandalas?), it is not itself the path. Yet it can awaken us to the fact that there *is* a path, suggest its nature, and give us some feedback about what it means to be on it. Astrology is, therefore, an aid; but walking the path is not a matter of concepts.

2

Images of Change: Astrology as a Symbol System

The most basic teaching of astrology, as well as its most basic assumption, is that all is change. At first sight this seems too obvious to mention. The ever-moving heavens embody the more general truth that everything is movement by its very nature. Astrology assumes that life on earth is mirrored in, synchronized with, and symbolized by the constant change of the heavenly bodies.

However, though we may accept omnipresent change as a principle, our tendency is often to think that change means that various solid things (i.e., planets, people, things) are in constant motion. This is quite different from assuming or accepting that *all* is change, that change is of the very nature of all supposedly solid "things," and that therefore there are no solid, ongoing "things" at all.

For example, we could say that Jupiter is a planet which is in motion. But it would be more accurate to say that Jupiter *is* motion, and that it is impossible to speak truthfully about Jupiter—of its mass, size, shape, color, and orbit—without referring to its movement. We may speak of it grammatically as a solid entity, but this is actually a convenience not supported by facts. Jupiter was born from movement, grew in movement, and continues to be what it is only by virtue of its movement, from the molecular to the galactic level.

We could go one step further and speak of the nature of the atom, or even of subatomic processes. Atomic physicists now see matter itself as being basically motion; when you try to touch its "thingness", its solidity vanishes like a mirage. The atom itself is seen as movement, and the solid things we can touch merely seem so because their movements are not discernible by our senses.

This idea of omnipresent, pervasive change is not new. It forms the basis of the Chinese *I Ching* (Book of Changes), just as it underlies the entire Nahuatl-Mayan calendrical system. Of the latter, Frank Waters, contemporary novelist and ethnographer, writes:

> One of the most fascinating Nahuatl hieroglyphs is *Ollin*, Movement. It is the seventeenth of the twenty day-signs in the Sacred Calendar of the Nahuas and Mayas...
>
> The hieroglyph is basically simple, consisting of two entwined lines. There are many variations. The lines may be straight or curved, thin or blocked. One may be colored red, the other blue. One version is that of a serpent and a centipede entwined. But simple as the hieroglyph is, its meaning is profound. It symbolized the interlocked polarities of the cosmic dualities; earth and sky, light and darkness, male and female, good and evil. The tension between them was what gave movement, life, to man and the universe.[1]

It embodies, then, "the Nahuatl premise of movement and change underlying all existence."[2]

In the Buddhist tradition, the omnipresence of change is fundamental. In her small, precise booklet *The Secret Oral Teachings in Tibetan Buddhist Sects*, Alexandra David-Neel wrote:

> The tangible world *is* movement, say the Masters; not a collection of moving objects, but movement itself. There are no objects "in movment," it is the movement which constitutes the objects which appear to us: they are nothing but movement.[3]

This general principle is contained in the Four Noble Truths which are the foundation of Buddhist practice. The Buddha

said that all is suffering (first Noble Truth) and that suffering
results from craving (second Noble Truth). This craving is to
have something fixed, some solid reference point which we
feel we can count on or possess, which might secure our sense
of self, make our ego seem solid. But the Buddha was quite
unequivocal in stating that "everything composite is transi-
tory." This transitoriness results in suffering because we resist
it. Ego wishes to set itself apart from the ongoing omnipresence of change. It (that is, each of us) wishes to be some*thing*.

Chogyam Trungpa, Tibetan meditation master and scholar, explains the relationship between impermanence, ego, and
suffering:

> The effort to secure our happiness, to maintain ourselves
> in relation to something else, is the process of ego. But this
> effort is futile because there are continual gaps in our seem-
> ingly solid world, continual cycles of death and rebirth,
> constant change. The sense of continuity and solidity of self
> is an illusion. There is really no such thing as ego, soul, or
> *atman*. It is a succession of confusions that create ego.[4]

Astrology is quite consistent with these teachings in a number of ways. First, the astrological symbolism demonstrates
"continual cycles of death and rebirth, constant change" both
in the signs and houses themselves,* and the never-ceasing
movement of the planets through those signs and houses, meas-
uring the unceasing flux and pattern of experience and consciousness. Second, the symbolism contains "gaps" in the
changes of sign, but more pervasively in the fact that the implications of astrology serve to undercut our assumptions about
the solidity of our world.

Astrology, then, accepts—and is even based on—the notion that there is no solidity or permanence except what we
attempt to create through use of our concepts and conceptual
frameworks, which by their very nature tend to ignore the
flux they attempt to encapsulate.

One of these frameworks is the astrological birthchart itself, and astrologers should use some care in how they consider it. The birthchart takes the ongoing flux of the heavens
and takes a sort of "stop-action" photograph from the perspec-

---

*See the glossary for an explanation of a horoscope.

tive of earth. It is easy to forget the ongoing "action" from which a stop-action photo is taken, say, at a sports event. In terms of ego, such a stop-action may reinforce the idea that there is something solid, a self-reference point, in the ongoing flux of experience.

As with a photograph, the birthchart can reveal character, and obviously it has an aspect of truth to reveal. But ego would like continually to reentertain itself with its own stop-action photograph and to ignore the illusion that this embodies. In the "real game," as in life, there is no stopping. One must sit exposed to the elements and take part. One can too easily become habituated to living life second-hand.

In other words, these astrological "snapshots" too easily become fixed reference points. People too easily ignore that the birthchart is, from an astrological perspective, merely the universe's expression of a specific time and place, seen from a specific perspective (geocentric), and recorded through certain accepted traditional symbols placed on a flat page. We should recognize, first, that the procedure we follow—isolating a moment in ongoing time—will influence what we discover through it; and second, that the image presented *is* only that moment in ongoing change.

In our age the public view of events is defined by images isolated from the changing context of complex situations. It is a temptation to consider the birthchart in a similar way instead of in its true nature as a child of movement. Because its true nature *is* as a child of movement, a chart should be considered within a context of movement. One way of doing this is by the practice of planetary progressions, transits, and other techniques of astrological time analysis.* Though these techniques use the birthchart as a fixed point of reference, they add the consideration that the meaning of the chart at any time is imbued with ongoing change.

The birthchart is, in one sense, a display of the planetary transits at any time of birth. Considering it in this way is helpful because just as a transit to a natal chart may "give birth" to a particular cycle of experience, so the birthchart

---

*See the glossary for an explanation of progressions.

itself gives birth to a cycle of experience. In the case of the birthchart, we refer back to the starting point and tend to see solidity there, whereas with a transit we don't generally assume that the beginning of the cycle is anything solid, except insofar as we become attached to the experience developed through the cycle.

Another way of integrating change into the horoscope is to realize that the astrological symbol systems themselves are indications of process. Not only that, but the processes thus symbolized imply, through the fact of their movement, the insufficiency of fixed reference points. More specifically, astrological symbols describe, in different ways, the ongoing process of "ego-ing." (Ego here becomes an intransitive verb: "to ego.") They indicate what we *do*, not what we are.

I am referring here to the three major groups of astrological symbols: the planets, signs, and houses. Each group—or each symbolized process—contains within itself the notion that the solidity of one's self-conception and self-assumption must eventually be broken apart, dissolved, and transformed. Furthermore, these transformations may be seen as quite natural, even "organic," as they are not only congruent with other life processes (as indicated in particular through the signs, with their seasonal emphasis), but are actually implied by the initial statement of separation itself.

In other words, in the very statement insisting on separation, a chain of causal movement is set off which leads, through its own inner logic, to its own negation. In this sense, ego is "made to be transformed." Ego's insistence on its own separation, centrality, or fixity is symbolized differently in the planets, signs, and houses; but in each case there is a clear process through which ego extends outward and then, by extention of that same energy, undergoes change. The astrological symbols show the different ways in which ego implies its own opposite.

The delineations which follow are not intended in any way as complete treatments of the symbols involved. I have attempted to sift from the many symbolic associations of the signs, planets, and houses those core meanings which most clearly demonstrate the egoing process. The treatment of the planets is given first, as it is the most involved, and because I think their meaning is more evident than with the signs and houses—perhaps because the planets represent psychological factors which are more easily attributable to ego. The signs are given next because the houses, which follow, can then be explained as a parallel rhythm.

The reader should keep in mind that in each case the process begins with a symbol of separation: the centralized solar impulse; the separatist tendencies of Aries; and the ascendant with its connection to the individual, separate body.* These provide three obvious attributes of ego, for the egoic process begins from a separatist standpoint, stressed either as a starting point for potency or radiation (the Sun), or simply as a constant picture of essential separation from others, or separation from experience itself (the ascendant). From its separatist standpoint, ego then claims, explores, and expands its territory until, by continuing the attempt to secure its ground in ever more solid and enduring forms, it ends up negating itself. The planets, signs, and houses provide three perspectives on how this occurs.

We should also realize that many people refuse to accept or fail to recognize this logic. Ego will do almost anything to keep itself solid, to perpetuate the illusion of its own viability. On a psychological level, this is what lies behind the view that the three outermost known planets (Uranus, Neptune, and Pluto) are often experienced as collective energies.† Saturn, the Lord of the World, or Lord of the Realm of Ego, does not allow them into his realm if he can prevent it. For ego to include these energies would mean its own negation; but as we know, natally or by transit these energies make themselves known. The phenomenal world has its messages, however cryptic its language.

In a sense, egoing is like the snake eternally devouring its

---

*See the glossary for an explanation of the ascendant.

†The relationship between the collective and transformational manifestations of Uranus, Neptune, and Pluto is examined in Chapter Five.

own tail; it constantly negates itself. But it is so busy trying to feed and enlarge itself by devouring its world that it never really achieves perspective on its situation. As a wisdom system, astrological symbols can provide such a perspective. My hope is that the following material will help the reader see astrology—and ourselves—from such a perspective.

The Solar Impulse and the Planets

The process of development symbolized by the planets may be seen as indicating ego's continual attempt to feel and radiate from a sense of solid centrality, to expand, and then to crystallize the expanded territory. The ways in which this crystallization breaks down this attempt finally reveal that the original sense of solid centrality was only an illusion. The planets are seen here as psychological factors, energies which are part of the human makeup at this stage of evolution, as well as factors which can contribute to evolution beyond that stage. (Such evolution would be symbolized by the discovery of a planet beyond Pluto.) Taken together, the planets form a picture of the psychological process of creating ego, then of going beyond it and breaking it down by a threefold process of transformation. The starting point of the process is ego's desire to have and hold to a solid, central reference point, the Sun.

The notion of solidity at the center needs emphasis. Ego does not ask only for centrality but for solidity at that center. This is symbolized by the Sun as the center of the solar system *and* as something solid. Taoists speak of the center of a wheel which is valuable because it is empty,[5] but such a statement will not support our usual notions of ego. One may be "centered," in a sense, without having solidity in the middle, and it even seems that energies in motion (i.e., all energies) need to have emptiness in the middle if they are to be in motion at all. This notion of emptiness in the middle is what is central to the Taoist art of T'ai Chi.

This principle applies to human experience, where a solidified sense of self usually inhibits the flexibility necessary to adapt to ever-changing circumstances and to the fluidity that allows growth in the fullest possible manner. Physically, this is indicated by the sun, which though it seems solid, is really molten matter (possibly in a plasma state) in a condition of ceaseless change and release of energy. If the sun were solid, it would be cold. The fact that it is *not* solid is inseparable from its gift of ongoing energy. Reflected in these physical facts is the truth that a solid center is antithetical to the life-giving process.

Just as the sun seems solid, so the ego seems solid, even though both, upon examination, turn out to be processes instead of permanent entities. From this solid perception of sun and ego—a perception so bright that it can blind us—we begin the process of egoic aggrandizement symbolized by the planets.

Astrologically, the Sun symbolizes one's conscious will, one's strength, dignity, and creative radiation. This radiation extends itself farther and farther outward until the movement breaks down and the process of aggrandizement flips into one of fragmentation and undoing, and eventually into repolarization, new birth and new life.

In its manifestation as solid centrality, then, the Sun is a symbol of ignorance. This is true, even though it also stands as a symbol of enlightenment—of light that shines on all creatures and within all minds, undifferentiated and clear. This is not a contradiction, because the Sun symbolizes the notion that the same energy that produces ignorance (promulgated symbolically through the inner planets*) can lead to enlightenment, or *is* enlightenment, but unrecognized, due to the blinding flash of ego's assumption of centrality, or basic arrogance. As will become clear, these two aspects of the Sun are the same energy approached from two angles.

To discover this truth about the nature of ego requires a journey. In the Zen Buddhist tradition, for example, a student must go through a long process of meditation in order to discover that enlightenment has been within him all along. The student who travels a long way to visit the Master is told,

---

*See the glossary for an explanation of the inner planets.

"Open your own treasure house and use those treasures."[6] Still, the searcher had to travel a long way along the path to discover that he needn't have left, or even that there was no path. This path is symbolized by the planets, which are in one sense the components of man. Without man there is no journey, and without experience it becomes senseless to speak of one's enlightenment. (We should remember, however, that experience by no means requires a reference point.)

There is a Sufi story which teaches the same principle: The Sage tells the student to go seek the happiest man in the world and ask him for his shirt. Only when the student accomplishes this will the Sage teach him. So the student goes off on his search. He finds some happy people, but each tells him that, though he is a happy man, there is certainly one happier. Eventually, after much discouragement, the student comes to a man who admits to being the happiest man in the world; but when the student asks for his shirt, the man points out with a good laugh that he does not have one. The student, much confused at this point, then asks the man what he should do. The man then takes off the turban whose end had been shading his face. He is none other than the Sage himself. The student, when he recovers from his surprise, asks the Sage why he had not told him this years earlier, before his long journey which now seems so senseless. The Sage replies, "Because you were not then ready to understand. You needed certain experiences, and they had to be given to you in a manner which would ensure that you went through them."[7]

The journey from the unenlightened Sun to a more enlightened awareness begins with movement out from the center. The conscious and centralized will of the Sun does this by aggrandizing itself with habit patterns, security, and emotion. These are all symbolized by the Moon, the reflected light of the Sun. Habit patterns, rooted in the subconscious, may be said to "reflect" the Sun-ego because, being subconscious, they are the unedited results of the Sun's ongoing effort to establish its own solid centrality. (The Moon is also the "home" which, as in the Sufi story, one must leave in order to learn.

One must also leave that which gives light and warmth to this home—the centralized Sun.)

It becomes evident why soli-lunar afflictions, seen in this way, are often more growth-producing than more flowing angles. In the square and opposition,* the unconscious will challenges the conscious will, resulting in a dynamic tension. Ego's game becomes more difficult to maintain smoothly. The opposition phase can result in objective awareness of the way the conscious ego results in subconscious habit patterns which are by their nature not creative. The square aspect leads one toward a search for structure—either tangible or in consciousness—which will enable one to work with energies that pull in different directions. One such structure could be a spiritual search or the "treading of the path." In either case, one sees that one is *not* a solid entity or a seamless fabric, but rather different energies that happen to be found together.

In addition to being the Sun's "other half" (the subconscious consort of the masculine Sun), the Moon is also the ruler of organic form. The conscious will needs organic form to confirm its centrality. The Moon—whether at the level of habit pattern or organic form—gives the Sun something solid to stand on. This central arrogance supports itself in the world of forms, knowing that of itself it is not a solid thing. The Moon, on the other hand, being cold and lifeless, takes on the semblance of life through the Sun.

On another level, purity and strength need reactions and the sensitivity of emotion. The Moon is, in all this, the first and primary reflection of the solar impulse, leading some astrologers to refer to it as "personality," described as "the many-faceted vehicle through which the individuality (Spirit) expresses itself."[8] This is quite apt if we consider the Sun as "Individuality," etymologically indicating something which is "not divisible," which we would generally take to be synonymous with "solid." But emptiness is just as "indivisible" as any solidity and is much more congruent to the Sun as a creative spirit, because as we have seen, solidity is not creative. Ego, however, feels more comfortable with the solidity of form.

---

*See the glossary under *Aspects* for an explanation of square and opposition.

It is also worth noting that, though ego would like to be both solid and creative, modern astronomical discoveries and speculations indicate that even apparent solidity is an end product, with emptiness more of a creative indication. White holes (in theory) are empty sources of creation, whereas black holes are incredibly dense and absorb light.

In addition to the habit patterns, the thinking process also reinforces ego's sense of solidity. This is symbolized by Mercury, circling around the Sun, never going far from it, filling in all the gaps as (from Earth's perspective) it shuttles back and forth from one side of the Sun to the other. This is an indication of our mental activity, which serves both as a primary outlet for ego's outward extension and to convince ego that it is acting intelligently. The term "serve" is appropriate because Mercury has often been called the "servant" of the Sun. The function of a servant is to allow the master to remain convinced that there are no gaps in his seemingly solid world, no seams in the tapestry he projects out and continually weaves. Our thought-chatter does this for us, first by filling in any gaps or doubts with information, and second by seeing to it that the information is of a type (i.e., intelligent) that seems to honor the ego with its humanness. Thus, ego feels that it's "doing okay," acting appropriately for one of its kind.

From habit and thought, the egoing process moves to the development of a value structure. Ego begins to decide what, in the emotional material of the Moon and the mental material of Mercury, is to be valued. This valuing is the function of Venus, as is the natural attraction to relationship, because one is attracted toward what one values. Ego begins to find a sense of well-being through accepting what it likes and rejecting what it dislikes.

So habit, logic, and valuing are seen as extensions and supports for the process of ego and also as actual steps in that process of extension. It is not that the energies of these three planets should be considered malefic in themselves, but simply that they are usually approached from the wrong direction, or seen from the wrong angle. (We might say facetiously that ego "always has an angle," which is its own maintenance.)

In this chapter and those that follow, a new approach is described, but at present the concern is how ego promotes itself, since habit (the Moon) produces in each of us a characteristic type of neurotic activity. This is actually the flip side of the coin of an enlightened activity, which also might be produced. It is not necessary to reject habit per se, but rather to see how it serves to blind us to the ongoing game we all play and to our creative possibilities, which can emerge once we go beyond the limits of that self-enclosed game. Through the Moon we get so caught up in the game that we forget to look around at the playing field, or even beyond. Through Mercury, we develop an interest in the game and a sense of communication. Through Venus, we decide what we like and what we don't like in the game.

Once a value structure has been attained, ego feels free to act on the basis of its values. This action (which, in the metaphor, might seem to be winning the game) is symbolized by Mars. Mars is the first externalization, ego's first attempt to establish itself physically and actively as something distinct and recognizable in the world, a strength with which one may identify.*

The external thrust of Mars soon finds itself involved in social expansion and social context—the realm of Jupiter. Ego desires not only to go outward in a purely physical, unidirectional sense, but also to find social compensation through that outthrust, to expand its conquests through social ramifications, giving it a broader field of activity with which to identify. Simply put, ego desires to encompass more and more within its boundaries. If Mars is the act of conquering, then Jupiter is the expansion of territory that results, as well as that organized body of abstract justifications (which may be philosophical or religious) which gives credence and support to the conquering process.

---

*Mars is therefore to be distinguished from the Moon, Mercury, and Venus, which manifest primarily internally. These three are within or tied to the orbit of the Earth. This is not to say that Mercury has no outer manifestation or Mars no inner one, but simply that each has a *primary* reference. Mars, for example, is both inner aggression and outer action. Mercury is both thought and communication.

Having conquered and expanded, one needs to administer the territory, and Saturn is the process by which ego attempts to solidify what it has gained. Structures and limits are set to the aggrandizement, walls are raised to keep out intruders, and laws are passed to deal with internal chaos. Ego attempts here to secure its ground through such apparently fixed reference points as position, authority, and tangible reward. Thus, ego "establishes itself." Where the Sun is the illusion of solidity through reference to a centralized source of identity or energy, Saturn is the illusion of solidity through reference to tangible external references points.

Saturn is also ego's attempt to stop the outgoing radiation which so far has served to energize the whole egoic process. This turns out to be impossible, but Saturn's manifestation as a trickster arises to trick one's awareness into thinking that everything is static. This occurs through the creation of various fantasies or ways of structuring one's world, creating the illusion of solidity and permanence, which serve to convince one that everything is okay. While Saturn does not succeed in stopping the outgoing process, it does succeed often in tricking awareness. When the energy goes on outward (through the trans-Saturnian planets), and awareness is successfully tricked by Saturn's illusion of solidity, the three outer planets manifest primarily as collective agents. (Uranus, Neptune, and Pluto move so much more slowly than the inner planets that they hardly vary by sign in the birthcharts of millions of people born in the same month or even the same year. Hence, their energies are experienced collectively.) When the awareness is *not* tricked, there arises the possibility that these three planets can manifest as agents of transformation. (Here I deal with the trans-Saturnians as energies of transformation. In the next chapter the relation between this transformation and these collective indications is discussed.)

With Saturn, ego attempts to "establish itself"; but Saturn is only the limit of ego's conscious expansion, not the end of the basic energy radiation coming from the Sun. To continue the metaphor of conquering, expansion and solidification may stop, but the tribes that live beyond Saturn's walls have become infected by the whole process. We might say that ego has expanded into their territory and so has to deal with their energy, which seems to stand for everything ego does not. They are what ego defends itself against, and their way of life is quite naturally antithetical to ego's attempt to limit and order the world.

It is important to emphasize that Saturn represents basic insecurity, and that this insecurity is the same thing as ego's constant search for support through tangible reference points such as position and ambition. The message is that ego's "establishment" is an indication of basic insecurity. One attempts to secure territory because one feels inadequate, limited, insecure; and the height of one's battlements is in direct proportion to one's fear of the outlying tribes, who represent a freedom which ego finds threatening. The metaphor is instructive because this freedom is quite natural and to refuse to deal with these strategies is in some sense a resistance to a natural impulse.

When we go beyond Saturn, we may say that, though the solar impulse is still being promulgated, its nature undergoes a drastic change. In fact, the impulse, which coming out to Saturn has been continually trying to aggrandize and support one's sense of central, solid self-importance (Sun), now serves to break down that sense of central solidity. This drastic turnabout may seem strange, but it is actually quite natural. When any impulse of energy is taken to its utmost extension, it seems to flip over and change into its opposite. As an example, the athlete who is trained to top competitive condition is at greater risk of injury when he comes to his peak because he may be also closer to exhaustion. This is a fundamental principle of stress and is one reason for the rash of injuries just before or during major competitions.

On a more esoteric level, this principle is evident in the *I Ching* where a strong yang line changes to yin, and a strong yin line changes to yang. The *Ta Chuan (The Great Treatise)* tells us that "as the firm and the yielding lines displace one another, change and transformation arise."[9] So in the astrological system, as the energy of ego's amplification reaches its furthest extension at Saturn, it transforms into its opposite, the energy of ego breakup, dissolution, and transformation.

The drastic change that occurs between Saturn and Uranus is therefore the logical extension of ego's ongoing attempt to secure its ground. The logic, however, is not syllogistic but simply the way things work, the way energy manifests, which involves transformation. The fool in his persistence is beginning to become wise.

With the introduction of the trans-Saturnian planets, ego must become receptive to some sort of message from beyond its own sphere. Uranus is an apt symbol for initial receptivity, its glyph (♅) looks oddly like a radar antenna, ready to receive some sort of message. Uranian receptivity is primarily mental or intuitional, the power of intuitional insight to break down or to go through Saturn's walls and defenses. Though Uranus is receptive in that it receives messages that serve to break through Saturn's walls, it is quite active in the actual breaking through. As an antenna, it both receives and transmits energy and information. It breaches Saturn's walls much as television transmission passes through the walls of a house.

Through breaching these defenses, Uranus brings us new information, the new Idea, which may be anything from specific insight into how things (e.g., ego) work, or simply the fact that there is space beyond our fortifications—space, greater life, and a new kind of freedom. Because we are so used to our battlements, we tend to think that anything out there is an enemy. From the standpoint of ego—from the royalty of the Sun to the bureaucracy of Saturn—Uranus probably *is* an enemy. To the bureaucracy of Hamlin, so was the Pied Piper.

Uranus is sometimes visible to the unaided eye. This correlates with the fact that transformative agents or energies can be received by a conscious mind that has been told or trained where to look. To continue the metaphor of fortification, the "enemy" can be seen by the sentries if they know where to look, which probably means that they've been taught something about the way the enemy acts, or something of his nature. In other words, the initial insight that can break through ego is not something wholly unknown, since conscious awareness of intuitive insight and the messages of transformation coming from the world require some training, disciplined learning, and a positive use of Jupiter's and Saturn's energies. To sentries who know nothing of the natives or the outlying woods, the enemy remains hidden except for his arrows.

Uranian insight can become a tool which we can use to break holes in our solidified view of ourselves and the world we have created around us. It is not, however, a tool that ego controls. It is more powerful than ego, like a lightning bolt. So ego's "use" of this energy is not so much a matter of doing something with it as of coming to know its nature and to accept the truth of what it reveals.

What is actually happening with Uranus is that insight—not our own, but that which belongs to no one—is percolating through our world. Just as in the 1960s when the energies of change moved electrically through American society, or in the period between 1770 and 1790 when the ideals of individual liberty, equality, and brotherhood bubbled up in geographically distant places, so today intuition quickly networks through our individual psyches and nervous systems, breaking apart old crystallizations and bringing powerful messages from the world.

Once Uranus has breached the walls, or at least put holes in them so that one is aware of the creative space beyond, the waters of Neptune come through to inundate ego's pretended stasis, washing away the fragments of what ego thinks it should be or believes it is. Psychologically, Neptune is the power of a more encompassing, even unlimited vision. This may take the form of compassion or artistic inspiration, even mysticism. In any case, there is likely to be some form of idealism, which can be either positive or negative.

Neptune often manifests as a realization that one is not separate from others, that all are immersed in the same emotional totality. On a collective level, it is an indication of emotional tone as seen in such areas as fashion or trends in taste (e.g., popular music). On an individual or developmental level, it symbolizes an energy that eats away the Saturnian walls like acid. Presenting a more encompassing vision through yearning or inspiration, it enables one to see those walls in their true light as small, limited, and impermanent. One senses something greater which does not recognize the separate ego at all; and though this may remain as unconscious yearning in many, we could say that even those who live behind a high seawall know the power of the sea simply by feeling it.

Neptune brings a deeply felt desire and need for oneness on an emotional level: hence its association with mysticism, artistic inspiration, and narcotics, for each of these expressions is a search for oneness through diffusing the ego. In this way the yearnings of Neptune differ from those of the Moon, for the Moon accepts the separate ego and gives a yearning for one separate ego to find a place or a person to which to belong. The Sun's emphasis on separate individuality seems limited; the light of the Sun's individuality is, from the standpoint of Neptune, somewhat dim. To the man who has had a vision of Heaven, the "normal" earthbound reality is no longer satisfying. Such a person may feel compelled to see heaven within what others call daily life, or to see the spiritual potential within individual egos who are caught in their own nets. A person with such a vision may carry on with the quotidian for a while, but the vision will eventually eat away at his contentment. His desire to shore up ego's walls and defenses has been undermined by the power of what he has seen.

After Neptune's realization that ego is not ultimately separate, the energies of Pluto become increasingly important. Neptune symbolizes the giving up or sacrifice of ego's compulsions due to an attunement to an ideal or to the infinite. It does not, however, symbolize ego's radical death or the power of rebirth that naturally follows. Nor does it recognize the transformative power of the emotions. On a subtle level, Neptune remains dualistic: there is the ideal and the non-ideal, and however much the ideal may bring about a dissolving of all the walls, there is still some notion that the spiritual-ideal is distinct from the temporal-carnal. One may see the spirit in the flesh, but even then they are distinct. Pluto does not recognize such distinctions, and through this bringing together of essential polarities, power is released.

Pluto symbolizes great, transformative power stored in small places, such as in seeds or eggs. It also symbolizes power that is released from breakdowns (fission) and complete union (fusion). The potentiality of complete union implies that the entire world is empowered by the archetypal fusion of polarities. Sexual energy is one obvious example. This interplay of polarity results in movement and transformation. Pluto also symbolizes the power that transforms energies or entities from one state of being to another. One such transformation is from matter to energy (as with plutonium); another is from life to death, or death to life. The power released in such transformations can completely alter the face of the world, either physically with plutonium or psychologically with, for example, the tremendous emotional energy released through sexuality. In either case, the seed of the transformation (e.g., a small amount of plutonium) can result in a change which seems disproportionate to its size.*

Plutonian transformation is beyond the power of ego. The example of plutonium is an appropriate one because, though an ego may begin the chain reaction of a plutonium bomb or nuclear reactor, the ego cannot control what happens once the reaction is underway. This is evident not only in the reaction itself but also in the further reactions that come from it. The sad history of nuclear reactors shows that human controls simply do not seem sufficient. More pervasively, the history of the world since Alamogordo, with the spread of nuclear weapons all over the globe, may be seen as a continuation of the initial chain reaction of the first bomb. This is parallel to Pluto's influence in the psychological realm, which results in pervasive change that begins from apparently small sources. A negative manifestation of this is the tendency of many Pluto-

---

*Some astrologers may notice some similarity between Pluto and Mercury. Mercury is also associated with the interplay and union of polarities, with movement and change. The difference is that Pluto deals with emotions and Mercury more with thought. Nevertheless, the two planets have many parallels, as their glyphs suggest. Both are agents of transformation.

dominated people to nurse small wounds until they poison the personality; more positively, such people can be extremely resourceful, able to make a lot from a little, and able to transform themselves through the power of their emotions.

Human, egocentric control over these processes is an illusion. The power of Pluto does not come from the Sun but from the dark and fathomless nature of transformation itself. An example of such a transformation is what the Buddha called "a turning about in the deepest seat of being."[10] This turning about cannot be willed; if the ego wills it, it cannot happen. One needs to die to the will of the ego to release the power of such change, which sets in motion the chain reaction of enlightened activity or enlightened mind. The working of enlightened mind is itself a fusion of polarities: wisdom (Sanskrit, prajna) and skillful means (Sanskrit, upaya) unite in activity which is by its very nature world-transforming.

The notion that Pluto symbolizes a "turning about" points to a change in the direction of energy flow. Up until now, the outward movement of the solar impulse has been traced. After Pluto's turning about, there is movement back toward the Sun; but only because there has been, with Pluto, a critical reorientation. The radical death of ego needs to be complete, for only then will it be cathartic. The journey back to the Sun is not toward any sort of solid centrality of ego, but toward the constantly working light of enlightenment. The Sun is now the light of Mind, which simply shines, without reference point or judgment; the impartial light of warmth and generosity can be impartial and generous because it is now without reference point and hence not ego-bound.

As we will see during this journey, this Mind is beyond duality. It is therefore not concerned with its separation or self-importance, and therefore not concerned with its sense of solidity as a distinct "thing." The lack of reference point allows the Sun to experience its own true nature as a nonsolid source of energy for others. It takes its place in the company of other stars, doing what stars are "designed" to do.

Pluto is an energy source for the journey. The ego has been completely reoriented, looking again toward light, completely transformed. It is no longer ego as something distinct but simply energy making a journey. As an energy source, Pluto is again seen in its connection to atomic energy, the same energy that powers the Sun toward which we travel. Similarly, just as Pluto indicates abundant energy from small, potentially harmful sources, so the Sun is small in comparison to the solar system it empowers. The end and the beginning are linked; the Sun and Pluto are the ends of another polarity which higher consciousness brings together.

The first stage in the return from Pluto is symbolized by the selfless compassion of Neptune, seen not so much as a stage in the transformation of ego, but in a more positive, active focus. It is not that ego is subjected to Neptunian dissolving, but that enlightened energy now manifests through compassion, selflessly.

Selfless compassion is then connected with intuitive insight and the Idea of Truth. This Idea networks through the pathways of the world (Uranus), again in a more active focus, and finally becomes solidified into tangible structures (Saturn) that make it more lasting. These structures, still based on an energy that is not referring back to ego, then expand through society to enrich people and amplify their sense of the worth of living and of knowledge (Jupiter). On the basis of this richness, and having the knowledge of egolessness (Uranus) promulgated in writings (Jupiter here becoming sutras or sacred texts), human beings can develop a new approach to both action (Mars) and valued relationship (Venus). In both cases, the energy is based in compassion and a sense of totality rather than any central reference point.

In the final stages, confusion is clarified, dualities are seen as unity, and perception becomes clear (Mercury). Habit patterns and emotions (Moon) are seen to be essentially an expression or reflection of basic enlightened Mind (Sun). Both the full moon and the sun are traditional symbols of this enlightenment. They represent qualities that are within us all the time, but which go unrecognized because of the blinding of ego. We find that we have been seeing things from a wrong point of view, perhaps simply because we have been seeing things from any point of view.

Chiron and the Teacher as Transformer of Ego

The process described above sees ego's transformation as an extension of ego's aggrandizement: transformation comes about when the basic energy of solar radiation extends beyond the limits of Saturn. It seems, according to this logic, that ego is *meant* to be transformed. And yet, this poses an obvious problem. If transformation is organic and natural, then why do so many of us remain imprisoned by the fantasy worlds of ego?

It seems as if there is a gap to be bridged between Saturn and Uranus. That is, the solar radiation seems to flow quite generally, in everyone, out to Saturn; and, once the transformational process has been engaged, the progress of energy from Uranus through Neptune and Pluto also seems to flow quite naturally. Yet for most people, the change from Saturn to Uranus results in the solar radiation becoming unconscious, so that the trans-Saturnian planets are usually experienced as collective energies, rather than symbols of transformation.

It was noted above that Uranus is sometimes visible to an unaided eye, symbolizing that "transformative agents or energies can be received by a conscious mind that has been told or trained where to look." How shall we bridge this gap and acquire the training to receive this energy? How shall we know where to look to recognize the possibilities for insight and transformation in our lives?

If we are to follow astrological symbolism in seeking our answer, there should be some key between Saturn and Uranus to help us in bridging this gap. If we look there, we find the minor planet (or planetoid) Chiron, which orbits the sun between Saturn and Uranus. The symbolism is appropriate, because two key words often used with Chiron are "key" and "bridge." One of its two glyphs ($\mskip$) looks somewhat like a key.

Mythologically, Chiron was a centaur who served as a

teacher of many of the great warriors of Greece.[11] He taught not only the art of warriorship but also healing, philosophy and music. As the offspring of Kronos/Saturn, he was half-god. Some modern astrologers have found the meaning of Chiron to parallel his mythological background, thus connecting him with healing and teaching.

The term "teaching" needs to be understood in a particular light, as does the term "warriorship." To teach someone to be a warrior is not necessarily to teach him how to fight military battles alone. From a spiritual standpoint, the enemy is ego; the warrior needs to battle his own resistance to the spiritual process. This resistance is embodied to a great extent in Saturn, and thus Chiron may be seen as forming a bridge from Saturnian egoic limitations to the insight of Uranus.

The implication, then, is that we need teachers—people of true spiritual insight—to enable us to bridge the gap between our insecurities (Saturn) and our insight (Uranus), between ego's defenses and the sudden flashes that break them apart. We need to be told that such a thing is possible.

It is interesting to see the similarities between the meaning of Chiron and some of the similes traditionally assigned to the "spiritual friend" or teacher in Buddhism. In *The Jewel Ornament of Liberation*, a Tibetan text of the twelfth century which speaks about various stages of the spiritual path, we find:

> The "similes" are that spiritual friends are like a guide when we travel in unknown territory, an escort when we pass through dangerous regions, and a ferry-man when we cross a great river.[12]

At other times the teacher is likened to a physician and a warrior. We can see the parallel to the symbolism of Chiron: physician, warrior, bridger of gaps, mediator. The implication is that, according to astrological symbolism, a teacher is needed in order to bridge the gap between transcendent energy and our ego's limitations.

It might be noted, finally, that some astronomers do not consider Chiron to be an original member of the solar system, but to have come from outside of it, having been captured by the gravity of the system. This is symbolically parallel to the idea that Bodhisattvas voluntarily return to the world of suffering to assist others on the path to enlightenment. * It is as if they are drawn by the gravity of ego, a gravity which is due to ego's heaviness, its assumption of solidity.

Chiron, then, serves as a catalyst enabling the natural human energies to manifest more fully. Its discovery in 1977 seems extremely important for the modern age, as we try to recall our harmful projection of the energies of Uranus, Neptune, and Pluto and make them conscious facets of our spiritual growth instead of potentially destructive facets of the phenomenal world. This question is discussed further in the fifth chapter.

The other planets are apparently part of the original solar system and part of the generic makeup of man. Their order implies that the same energy which produces ego also produces ego's transformation.

Those who have read Dane Rudhyar's *The Sun is Also a Star: The Galactic Dimensions of Astrology* (New York: Aurora Press, 1975) may feel that there is a major disagreement between the point of view expressed in that book and the one expressed here. Rudhyar states that the trans-Saturnian planets owe allegiance to the galaxy, not to the Sun, whereas here they are described as steps in human growth symbolized by the path of solar radiation. The former seems to imply "outside help," the latter emphasizes inner work, or the power of transformation inherent in man as presently constituted.

A closer examination of spiritual practices reveals that these two are not really contradictory. We may take an example from the Buddhist tradition. On the one hand, there is great emphasis placed on students coming to understand their own

---

*In the Mahayana Buddhist tradition, the Bodhisattvas are human beings who have reached a state of enlightenment in which they are motivated by compassion to voluntarily reincarnate in the world to aid other sentient beings in their spiritual growth. This is accomplished through an inseparable union of wisdom and skillful means.

minds and patterns of neurotic attachment. The Buddha ex-
plicitly instructed his followers diligently to pursue their own
salvation, and further to:

> Believe nothing which depends only on the authority of your
> masters or of priests. After investigation, believe that which
> you have yourselves tested and found reasonable, and which
> is for your good and that of others. (Kalama Sutra)[13]

On the other hand, Buddhism places great emphasis on the
guru-student relationship and on the whole tradition of a
lineage of authorized teachers. These teachers not only serve
as catalyzing functions of Chiron but also embody the wisdom symbolized by all of the planets. To the Buddhist, the
guru must be an actual, external person to whom one can
relate but who does not speak for ego or centrality.

The two positions are reconciled because although the guru
is an outside agent—certainly from ego's point of view—he
is not someone who will simply say a magic word or confer
magical power on the student to bring about enlightenment
effortlessly. Unless the student is committed to individual effort, the guru's teaching and power falls on barren ground.
The need for individual effort and the view that enlightenment can be attained through individual effort is supported
by the following passage in *The Jewel Ornament of Liberation:*

> However, if you wonder whether dejected people like our-
> selves can ever attain by our own exertions this unsurpass-
> able enlightenment, liberating themselves from Samsara
> which is by nature bewilderment, you may be reassured
> by remembering that if enlightenment can be won by hard
> work, it must be within our reach; for in all beings like our-
> selves the Buddha-motive, Tathagatagarbha, is pres-
> ent...Tathagatagarbha embraces and permeates all
> beings.[14]

However, later in the same text, the author, Gampopa, stresses
the importance of the guru:

> ...although you may possess the most perfect working
> basis, but are not urged on by spiritual friends as a con-
> tributory cause, it is difficult to set out on the path toward
> enlightenment, because of the power of inveterate propen-
> sities due to evil deeds performed in former times.[15]

In a sense, the guru is both part of oneself and part of the external world. Still, Buddhist tradition places emphasis on an actual living guru, and in this sense we would say that "outside agents" are at work in the process of transformation. This parallels Rudhyar's notion that the outer, transforming planets have allegiance to galactic energies, not primarily solar ones, for the guru, though he may manifest the energy of any of the planets, is particularly significant as a manifestation of the energies symbolized by the trans-Saturnians.

This emphasis on "outside forces" is also found in the writings of P.D. Ouspensky, one of Gurdjieff's students. In *The Fourth Way*, Ouspensky uses the term "shocks," which are forces that enable one to keep to one's path at those points when it becomes quite easy to go off in another direction. Though he says that such shocks can come from oneself, from accident, or from others, the major emphasis seems to be that organized schools or groups help to provide them. Ouspensky explains the need for shocks:

> The only thing we need is shocks, but we cannot make them. Even if we think of them, we are not confident enough, we do not trust ourselves, do not know for certain that the shock will produce the desired effect. That is why organized work includes in itself so many shocks, so it is not left to ourselves. We are so fast asleep that no shocks wake us—we do not notice them.[16]

These examples should suffice to indicate that any program of spiritual development operates not only through individual work, but through some form of external teaching, catalyzing, or stimulus. The entire Christian tradition is based on such an external agent, the Christ, God-become-man, who came to save the world from itself. In the Old Testament, Yahweh constantly intervenes in the affairs of men, shocking them into awareness of their covenant with him and of their own true nature.

In terms of the planetary system, we may speculate that the outer planets are galactic in their affiliations. Yet in order to receive galactic messages it is necessary for an individual to work out his own salvation with diligence, and to do so with recognition of his own aloneness. In this way, one allows yang-oriented solar radiation to transform itself into the yin-polarity of the outer three planets. These planets are yin insofar as they are no longer promulgating ego's neurosis, but are open to receive transformative messages from one's experience; but they can of course be quite yang insofar as they force one to a great realization.

Ego's hold must be given up, but this does not mean becoming passive. In fact, giving up ego's hold turns out to be a release of energy, not its loss. There are energies within and around us far more powerful than those of ego. These transcendental or transegoic energies are symbolized by the outer three planets, and contact with them is often a humbling experience because we find that we (ie., ego) cannot coopt them, and if we fight them we lose. But this loss is—or can be—a very powerful victory. The humility we gain connects us to the true lineage of enlightened teachings. No matter how we view the matter, a complete picture of man must include energies which do not have primary reference to ego.

3

The Twelve Signs as Stages in a Process

The twelve zodiacal signs are readily related to the cycle of the seasons. The organic nature of this process is outlined clearly in Dane Rudhyar's *Astrological Signs: The Pulse of Life:*

> The essential thing about the Zodiac is not the hieroglyphs drawn upon celestial maps; it is not the symbolical stories built up around Greek mythological themes—significant as these may be. It is the human experience of change. And for a humanity which once lived very close to the earth, the series of nature's "moods" throughout the year was the strongest representation of change; for the inner emotional and biological changes of man's nature did correspond very closely indeed to the outer changes in vegetation.[1]

The relationship to organic, seasonal processes is also expressed in the *Book of Hours*, found in the Musée de Cluny in Paris, France, where the twelve signs are directly linked to the agricultural life of those who worked the land.

Because the zodiacal signs are directly associated with seasonal processes which we all observe constantly, the connection between growth and dissolution is quite evident. In relation to ego, however, this connection may be a bit harder to see, as the nature of the signs is somewhat abstract. In order to clarify the relationship, we must select a starting point: the vernal equinox and the sign of Aries.

One of ego's characteristics is its desire to separate itself from the matrix that gives rise to it. This separation is symbolized by the first sign, Aries, associated with the spring equinox, and therefore with plants pushing up through the matrix of the soil. Aries indicates the initial separation of each entity from the ground which supports it, the ground on which manifestation is based. In Alice Bailey's words, "Aries initiates the cycle of manifestation."[2] Thus Aries may be said to be separation, plus identification with being separate.

This separation is impulsive. The plant comes through the soil without considering whether it will be supported once it emerges. It does not consider whether it will be tended or watered. But once emerged, it realizes that its impulse may soon die if it is not supported by substance, or if it is not valued (and if it *is* valued, it will be supported by physical substance as a sign of that valuing).

Ego therefore begins to search for some way to secure itself. Psychologically, this means that it values itself; physically, it means that it feeds itself with substance. Ego's initial desire to be separate results in such insecurity that it seeks to secure itself through tangible physical attachment and values: separation and identification (Aries) are supported and apparently confirmed by substance and value (Taurus).

Both of these first stages imply duality: What is valued implies what is not valued. What is physically separate implies that from which it is separate. The third sign, Gemini, symbolizes these dualities, as well as the duality of the first two signs themselves. It also symbolizes the mental search for a way to relate or unify these dualities.

This mental search is an attempt to do away with doubt. Doubt arises from duality, from separation; and from the doubt of duality comes search or movement. This search through thought is symbolized by the first "human" sign because thought—the attempt to bridge dualities—is the first humanizing factor in the zodiac. Separation and support through substance are not specifically human but are plant and animal processes as well.

The wish to bridge the dualism and make everything solid and unitary again is the birth of thinking, the constant shuttle of mental activity which seeks to fill up any gaps in one's confidence. Thus, in Gemini separation and identification are supported and apparently confirmed by thought-speed.

Ego's next issue is security, symbolized by Cancer. There may be some sort of mental conviction of security, coming from having all gaps seemingly filled; but ego still feels that all is not well. Mental security is not enough; what is needed is an emotional sense of contentment, of shelter, of protection. When thought-speed does not make everything all right, the separative impulse seeks emotional satisfaction in insularity and habit patterns that bolster the feeling that one is not merely an impulse but some sort of self. The impulse clothes or covers itself with habit.

In other words, if thinking does not fill in all the gaps, habitual emotional responses attempt to do so. These habitual responses give an apparent sense that there is a self underlying any level of interaction. (This is a simplified version of Cancer. The significance of Cancer is considerably amplified in Chapter Six, though in a different context.)

Once the initial impulse has developed into this sense of personal security, then as ego it can create. From a deeply rooted sense of personal identity, ego is able and more than willing to radiate outward, just as a tree branches into the sunlight when its roots are secure. Cancer attempts to create a secure enclosure for ego, but the nature of ego is not merely to be enclosed but to shine and be admired. This is Leo, where separation and identification are apparently confirmed by a feeling of strength and an ability to create.

Having created, ego wishes to perfect its expression. This is one facet of Virgo. Just as Gemini provides a phase of adjustment after Aries and Taurus, so Virgo provides a phase of adjustment after Cancer and Leo. The sixth sign brings the critical faculty of mind to bear in order to perfect the self-expression. On the one hand, this perfecting is accomplished through establishing a proper relation between the inner emotions or subjectivities and the sense of natural, creative strength. On the other hand, perfecting occurs through awareness of the need to relate with others.

Virgo provides the realization that personal radiation or strength is essentially barren unless a person takes cognizance of others and adjusts his sense of self-importance and centrality in order to find true relatedness. It is worth noting that Leo is considered the most barren of all the signs; one is advised against planting when the moon passes through this sign. This barrenness is reflected here because if Leo does not extend itself to Virgo, all of its creations go for nothing. This is reflected in the planets by the fact that solar radiation, associated with Leo, first contacts Mercury, associated with Virgo. Without the planets, solar radiation does not result in life. Ego does not wish to be barren but to be fruitful and multiply itself. Virgo is the sign of the harvest, and in it separation and identification finally harvest the fruits of its separation, realizing that separation and identification are not sufficient unto themselves but need to perform some service. An adjustment is made so that ego's creations—another result of separation— can find a truer harvest in social function.

This social function is symbolized by Libra. Virgo might also be said to represent social function—as in service—but Libra is connected with weighing one's activities against a standardized social value.[3] In Libra, ego sees itself reflected in others. Here, as in its polar opposite, Aries, the issue is identity; and as in Aries there is also a question of separation. Two separate individuals form a relationship, and the basis of the relationship is that there are two separate individuals to relate. However, as indicated by the process of the signs, it seems that the true basis of relationship is the insufficiency of the isolated, even radiant ego. There is a need to form social units. Ego's separation seeks confirmation through one-on-one relationship in a socially valued context. Ego confirms itself through another.

This is a critical point, because we see ego's continued expansion beginning to become questionable. Ego needs to recognize the existence of others as equals. It is entering a realm where it cannot control the energy it encounters because that energy comes from others. Librans are notorious for their desire to please others, and Mars, ruler of the original Arien impulse, is in its detriment in Libra.* The impulse begins to lose its assurance.

The next step, which goes beyond the recognition of others as equals, is the recognition of their depth, symbolized by Scorpio. Dane Rudhyar describes the eighth sign as "the urge in the individual to merge in absolute union with other individuals in order to constitute together a greater organic whole."[4] This merging requires full recognition of the depth of others and their emotions; and complete union with another person on this level requires death of the ego, the old self-conception. This level of union, being complete, logically requires that the individual components lose their identity.

In the northern hemisphere, the yearly cycle of Scorpio is the time of death for organic life, the decaying of leaves into humus which will bring forth new life in the spring. Scorpio is the power of both death and rebirth, and also the recognition that this process releases (or is itself the release of) power. If Gemini is an attempt to bridge polarity mentally, Scorpio is the energy that fuses polarity emotionally, releasing tremendous regenerative power. This parallel between Gemini and Scorpio is symbolized by the similarity of the glyphs for their respective rulers: ☿ (Mercury) and ♇ (Pluto). The relationship between Mercury and Pluto is too complex to go into here, except to note that both are in some sense messenger figures. The tone and quality of the messages differ, but both imply unification.

In one sense, ego dies in Scorpio. This might seem to be the end of the process. It is not, however, for two reasons: First, the end of egocentric concerns on an emotional level—or the cessation of ego's demands—has not yet extended into the world. Second, this death is of the individual ego itself; but attachment may linger through environmental contact. It may even be rebuilt in some fashion. Extreme trauma sometimes results in a sort of "substitute" ego. Scorpio represents death, and through death, the possibility of genuine rebirth; but there is no guarantee.

---

*See the glossary for an explanation of detriment.

The ego may be seen as empty, dead; but it is necessary that the world also be seen as empty. The last four signs depict, at their highest manifestation, this growth toward seeing the world as empty, which involves emptying it of our preconceptions and self-preoccupation. On another level, we might say that Scorpio is the empty place of death, which can be continually experienced even in the midst of life; but there always seems to be a return to a world we take for granted. The final four signs can show us the insufficiency of such a point of view.

Sagittarius, the third mutable sign, is again a phase of adjustment and learning. Its emphasis is on systematic knowledge, abstraction, and the ability to gain a broader perspective on the Scorpionic process and how it developed from Libra. It therefore gives a perspective on these two phases (Libra and Scorpio) of human relationship with its social function and balance, then its depth and transformative power. The death of one's self-conception emerges out of relationship and is a highly turbulent issue. Sagittarius seeks an objective perspective, seeks to put the turbulence into the wider context of human advancement and learning. Sagittarius is an adjustment from the concerns of the individual to those of the wider whole, the recognition that after one has died to oneself, one must learn how to make that death part of one's mission.

Sagittarius is also expansion, and problems arise when the Scorpio phase has resulted in turbulence and release of power, while the lingering attachments of ego remain. The ego has seen its own insufficiency, but the process of grasping goes on nonetheless. The dark side of the Sagittarius-Scorpio connection is in expansion based on personal chaos: arrogance resulting from the fear of ego-death. The brighter side is that one adjusts to the Scorpionic release of power and seeks a life path of learning and expansion through which one can use Sagittarius-Scorpio for a wider human benefit. Thus, there is a necessary reformulation of purpose through taking a broadened and abstract perspective.

Capricorn is the result of this perspective; or, if such perspective accepts or is willing to work with the Scorpio power without reference to ego, Capricorn is mission in life. If Sagittarius is the conception of the mission and the mobilization of power towards its accomplisment, Capricorn is the organization of energies so that the abstractions can become realizable in the so-called real world. Negatively, however, Sagittarius is a stage at which the lingering attachments of ego reformulate their identity based on some sort of abstract purpose, which then secures its identity further through the tangible attachments of Capricorn. One becomes immersed in matter, in the structures of society, and the danger is that one will find identity through these structures to be even more solid than any that has existed heretofore. The danger is particularly acute, since Scorpio separates Capricorn from the necessary, balanced judgment of Libra. Positively, of course, Capricorn can be a sense of mission based on an expanded vision resulting from the death of one's self-conception.

These dangers are augmented because Capricorn follows the tremendously emotional and transformative power of Scorpio and the equally potent motive power of Sagittarius. Having lost oneself, one may become completely absorbed in any tangible advancements that are provided, with all of one's despair providing the impetus. Ambition and position create an entirely new illusion after the old one of an isolated, potent ego has broken down. Still, in its optimum expression, Capricorn can focus transformational motivation into a mission, a vocation. One's ego has died and been reborn (Scorpio) into a new field of action (Sagittarius) which takes tangible form (Capricorn).

In Aquarius any residual notions of the "doer" on a mission should begin to dissipate. Missions extend out into networks of human association and social vision. There is a new perspective of mission and it becomes clear that it is not one's *own* at all, but a mission in which one takes part as a member of a larger brotherhood. One works in and through the group, or through the power of the network, so that the idea of one's importance dissipates. The networks of Aquarius do not require, and hence do away with, the authority figures of Capricorn.

As a result, ego sees in Pisces that the mission is really the ongoing work, but even that is an illusion because one's motivation is inseparable from the work itself. In other words, it is no longer valid to think that "I have come so far as to be able to serve humanity by giving myself up in service to it," but rather that there never was any "I" to give. In Buddhist terms, "giver and receiver are one"; there is no giver, no one to give to, and no act of giving. The separation has always been an illusion. There is no other recourse but reabsorption from which one is never completely separate. The notion of separation is only a stage on the path, not a solid state of being.

The same could be said, of course, of the Piscean stage itself. Piscean absorption is no more solid or enduring than Arien separation. The main issue with Pisces is the sacrifice of a reference point. A reabsorption into what I have called the ongoing work necessitates this: any retention of the reference point indicates that one is working for oneself. Well-known Piscean compassion is similar: true compassion need not refer to itself or to any giver.

This compassion leads to the next cycle of manifestation, symbolized by the cusp between Pisces and Aries.* This is the Bodhisattva ideal of Buddhism, that instead of leaving the world after attaining liberation or nirvana, the Bodhisattva returns to it to lead others onto the same path of self-realization.

This, then, is the logical conclusion of Pisces: that one must sacrifice fully and give of oneself fully to the ongoing work, until all others become enlightened. One must therefore go into the world of separation again, into Aries, becoming now the Lamb of God who will lead others onto the path. On a psychological level, we cannot remain adrift with our ideals or illusions unanchored, but must go into action as one identified with those ideals. These ideals may manifest as compassion, or as dissipation or as alcoholism. These latter parallel compassion in that they may show a yearning for something better, a lack of solidity in one's self, and a tendency to be carried by something outside of oneself.

---

*See the glossary for an explanation of cusps.

So Pisces has two distinct manifestations, yet they are based on the common Piscean symbolism. On the one hand, absorption may indicate mere forgetfulness and giving up, so that the next cycle begins when one has forgotten the lessons of the old. In such a case, one goes on to repeat the old patterns of the zodiacal wheel: separation, valuing, thought-speed, and so forth, without any significant increase in awareness, at least on a conscious level. On the other hand, one may be absorbed through Pisces into the boundless waters of compassion and universalized consciousness, so that one begins the next cycle full of (soaked with) the lessons of the past. In this case, the next passage around the wheel is based on selflessness and a realization of the egolessness not only of oneself but of all others and of things. Quite likely, most of us find ourselves somewhere between these two manifestations, a position quite appropriate for a sign symbolized by two fish swimming in different directions.

The signs have been described in such a way as to emphasize ego's tangible outreach and its continual attempt to solidify its ground through obvious, tangible aggrandizement. The symbolism of the signs, being primarily seasonal, lends itself to such a materialistic explanation (whereas the symbolism of the planets, being more psychological, is not so much a tangible, time-generated process, but may be instantaneous).

It is important to recognize, however, that all of ego's attempts to secure itself reflect basic psychological drives. The process of the signs may be seen as moment-to-moment as well as lifetime-to-lifetime. Ego's driving mechanism is to emerge as something apparently solid and separate, to convince itself of its own security and rootedness, to empower itself through its creations and through relation to others. Thus ego extends itself into achievement and increased connections through that achievement; and it turns out that this same logic may lead ego to reach out so far that its integrity could change into either confusion or deep compassion. All of this may be seen within the insecure aggression that may exist in any given moment, in which one tries to establish oneself as a strong physical entity because of a deep feeling of groundlessness. Or one may be caught for a lifetime in the blind onrush of a never-ending treadmill of trying to establish one's solidity on every level but never quite succeeding. Or the process of the signs may describe the process of any individual life or series of lifetimes.

The wheel of energy described does not necessarily include value judgment. It may seem that the stage of Pisces is inherently more valuable than that of Aries, as the former is connected with selflessness and the latter quite readily is connected with self-centeredness. Both are connected with sacrifice. Whereas a person may be attached as easily to the conceit of "compassion" as to his conviction of separation, one sign is not inherently more valuable than another, either on a spiritual or temporal level.

Furthermore, every stage in the cycle is absolutely dependent upon every other. If there were no ignorance, there would be no enlightenment; if there were no separate beings, there would be no spiritual path. Piscean selflessness not only grows out of Arian separation; it is inseparable from it. The energy is simply in a different form.

The twelvefold sequence is summarized in a tabulation:

ARIES	where the separation and identification of the ego as it evolves in the tangible world begins. Initial separation leads to
TAURUS	whose supporting and confirming substance and value system leads to
GEMINI	where thought-speed attempts to fill all the gaps of doubt, which leads to
CANCER	where through emotional security one feels an "inner identity," which leads to
LEO	that extends ego through a sense of strength and creative power, which leads to
VIRGO	where the fruits of its separative creation are harvested. (They need a function and a social place or they become barren.) This leads to
LIBRA	where one relates to others and finds thereby a social function, leading to
SCORPIO	where the resultant death of one's sense of individual separation breaks down through the

power of relationship, through confronting the values of others, leading to

SAGITTARIUS where a necessary reformulation of purpose occurs through a broadened and more objective perspective. Ego's continued attachment through wider environmental contact leads to

CAPRICORN where dedication to some mission is a tangible commitment resulting from the previous reformulation of purpose. This leads to

AQUARIUS which expands the purpose through communication, becoming established, valued, pervasive. Purpose disperses identity through the group, leading to

PISCES which expands the purpose or mission until one realizes that the "giver" or "doer" is absorbed in it with no separation from the ongoing work. Absorption or reabsorption and consequent compassion lead back to separation (Aries).

4

The Twelve Houses and the Cycle of Outreach

The twelve houses of the horoscope are usually understood as twelve types or "fields" of experience;[1] twelve categories which comprise the round of mundane life. It is traditionally held that in these fields our energies become manifest, and in them we build our enduring sense of self. The term "houses" implies that these fields are separate from one another; houses are built of walls, and walls provide a sharp separation.

In practical terms, this separation is extremely useful. Astrological interpretation depends largely on the distinct meanings of its symbols. Nevertheless, there is pictured in the houses a *cycle* of outreach in which the individual houses are not only separate, but are also stages in a continuum. While it is true that character is formed or "built" in the distinct areas of experience symbolized by the houses, it is also true that these distinct areas taken together form a cycle in which each stage blends and develops into the next.

Because of this, the cuspal area between houses* is extremely significant, forming as it does an area of transition. This separation between houses is not a line of sharp demarcation but an area of gradually changing shade. In examining tran-

---

*See the glossary for an explanation of cusp and cuspal area.

sit cycles, this cuspal area becomes a period of time: the time the transitting planet takes to move through the cuspal area is the period of transition. In this way, we can see that the cyclic nature of the houses is not an abstraction, but is an indication of the ongoing process of our experience.

The study of the planetary transits through the houses shows the continuity of the house cycle. There is a shift in emphasis from one area of experience to the next, and this shift is related to the psychological energy of the transitting planets. But though the experience of each house is distinct, planetary transit cycles show a *continuity* of experience in which each stage develops naturally from the one preceding it. As a planet changes houses, we experience a clear shift in the focus of experience, yet the shift is part of a continuum; one stage prepares for the next. It is somewhat like traveling from north to south: the climate of New England is clearly different from that of Virginia, yet the change from one to another is gradual as certain types of vegetation take over from others.

An example of developmental continuity is the transit of Mars from the sixth house into the seventh. Mars in the sixth may indicate a period in which one directs energy (Mars) into tasks or work, or into working for others, into situations in which one serves another or is subservient in some way (sixth house). Because Mars indicates narrow ego focus (or a danger of that), this period can bring about a rising tension: the energy of Mars wants to be seen as potent, important, and be recognized in its own individuality. It chaffs when it is forced into service to someone else. As Mars moves into the seventh house, the tension may erupt into disputes, as one openly states one's own case or position. The seventh is a house of one-on-one relationships of equality. Mars is often expressed through anger; the seventh can be both "the other" and "open enemies." So after a period of putting oneself second in a way that does not quite "sit right," one's desire to state one's position and be recognized comes out into the open, either in an attempt to rebalance the situation (Libra's rulership of the seventh house) or as conflict with those perceived as "enemies." Though the two houses symbolize different experiences, they are both part of a natural cycle of growth and outreach.

The signs also depict a cycle of energy. The distinction between the signs and houses is that the houses symbolize a *personal* outreach, whereas the signs are more the archetypal pattern itself. That is, the houses of an individual horoscope are calculated from the precise moment of birth, and show how an individual faces and reaches out into his world in a distinctive way. Transit cycles may again be used to illustrate: the movement of planets from sign to sign symbolizes developments in the collective karma, a pattern experienced by everyone on earth; the movement of the planets through the houses indicates personal karma, the causal chain of one's personal outreach.

Because the houses make up a cycle of experience, they have form and pattern when taken together. Alexander Ruperti, contemporary astrologer and writer, describes this pattern in reference to the four quadrants of the horoscope, with the first quadrant as growth in essential being; the second quadrant as growth in the capacity to use more effectively the energy of a planetary energy; the third quadrant a period of growth in one's socially functional use of the energy; and the fourth quadrant a period of growth in influence via that energy.[2]

The pattern described here has many parallels to Ruperti's model. The main distinction is that Ruperti takes a humanistic approach and speaks of character-building from a broad base of non-judgmental human development. The point of view here is a bit narrower: the houses are seen as stages in personal ego-transformation—or stages in which our natural outreach into the world leads us toward a potential for letting go, and therefore transformation—and stages in outreach each of which contains the potential for letting go in that moment. This view does not deny that the houses depict personal and social outreach, but views this very outreach as potentially transformative. One implication is that true character-building includes, and even necessitates, the dissolving and transformation of ego, or that, ultimately, character is built most effectively when ego is allowed or encouraged to see that it can let go of its impetus for expansion. Another implication is that our personal world—the world we continually create through personal outreach—has immense teaching value because it follows a pattern that ends up in its own negation and dissolution. The issue is the teaching value of our own experience, that the world can awaken us to recognize our own insubstantiality.

Thus, the houses awaken us to the spiritual teaching value of our experience. The impulse of separate ego leads, by its own internal logic, to imprisonment; yet at the same time it contains the possibility for release.

We do not generally view our experience this way. Our world seems to be ruled by Saturn and the Moon. Saturn, the lord of this world, induces us to see it as a place to achieve our ambitions and solidify our sense of self through tangible achievement. To the ancients, the earth was the "sublunar realm," for the Moon is the ruler of organic form as Saturn is the ruler of structured form. The Moon also rules habitual patterns, and thus the world seems to combine habitual patterns with desire for achievement. But Saturn is a trickster, here as always, and the Moon a symbol of illumined mind. We need to look more closely at the realm ruled by these two planets and to distinguish the two aspects of its nature. It appears as a place to solidify our need to belong (Moon) into the tangible patterns of ambition (Saturn), but its hidden nature is a place where we can learn through discipline (Saturn) to recognize illumined mind even in our habit patterns (Moon). We can do this through our experience of the houses, because there, hidden behind the traditional interpretation of character-building, is a process which leads, by its own inner logic, to the dissolving of ego.

We shall find that this follows the same pattern as other astrological cycles. The first stage is a release of potential, a mobilization of power. In Rudhyar's terms, "Every cycle of relationship begins in an act of mobilization of power—the power generated by the union of two factors."[3] In the cycle of the houses, the two factors are individual and environmental, though naturally they become blurred at many points, for every house has internal, relational, and external levels;[4] symbolizing the fact that we cannot separate our world from our mind. The middle of every cycle is a point of fruition and awareness (or, negatively, destructive polarization). The end of a cycle is a period of dissolving, for the "tone"[5] of the impulse is dissipating, needing to be replaced by an increase of consciousness. Here it is ego that dissolves, with particular emphasis on loosening identification with separative, individual potency. The individual's power in the world, generated at the ascendant, must dissolve and become universalized. The alternative is imprisonment.

The first house begins at the ascendant and initiates the counterclockwise cycle of the houses. * The first house is associated with Aries, and the two are linked because the physical form (first house) is one's most obvious form of personal separation (Aries) from others. Symbolized here are physical appearance, bodily form, and temperament. Being just below the horizon, † the first house contains an "inner" energy, but it interfaces directly with the outer world. It is those inner qualities that appear directly to the outer world. As such, it is not "mere appearance," but more that sense of appearance one might see in the portraits of Van Gogh or Rembrandt, for example—one that contains a transcendent spiritual quality.

The first house shows temperament, that first tangible outreach into life, which indicates how a person most comfortably interacts with the world. It represents the field of ego in its initial separation, body and appearance (as distinguished from the Sun, which is not so much a physical indication as an assumption of a central point of radiation). The first house is also where ego dramatically identifies with its own simple acts of outreach. Here is where personal power mobilizes in a union between oneself and world at the simplest level, that of physical exchange. The first house can therefore be associated with breathing or "prana," the vital breath of life.[6]

The second house indicates the field of extension of those values which support temperament, the management of one's resources and resourcefulness to support one's initial outreach. The second house also provides the physical substance which nourishes the body. It represents ego insofar as ego upholds itself in these ways, developing a system of values and of phys-

---

*See the glossary for an explanation of the movement of the ascendant.

†See the glossary for an explanation of the position of the houses.

ical support to confirm its outreach, which in turn confirms its existence. Furthermore, it is ego's search for these kinds of support.

In the third house, ego extends itself further into experience through certain mental functions which strive to give ego objective verification of those values developed in the second house. It is also the immediate environment which supports the physical and spiritual resources of the second house, and which, through its acceptance of ego's motility, allows it to expand its own development. The implication is that ego builds its immediate world (or its mental version of that world, for the third house is mentally oriented) from its sense of valuation, its skill in accepting and rejecting associated with Venus, the ruler of the second house. In other words, astrological symbolism suggests that our perception of the immediate world (third house) is not so clear and objective as we would like to think but is imbued with a sense of values and basic survival needs, which most people are not even consciously aware of.

If the third house builds ego in the immediate environment of interactions and communications which involve it sufficiently that it can ignore the gaps in its conviction of solidity, the fourth house can provide the inner sense of security which develops from this conviction. Ego will attempt to find this security despite any underlying doubts about the seamlessness of the fabric it has woven. We might say that some inner sense of security acts as a support or prop for the flexible movements of the third house; but at the same time the immediate environment of interactions also serves as a support for the sense of self; and there is a point (the nadir) where the two merge. This implies that a sense of "who I really am" which lies beneath any level of social interaction cannot exist by itself, but must be participatory. The inner identity symbolized by the fourth house can be a sense of rootedness and solidity, which in itself is an illusion that resulted from the third-house shuttle of trying to fill up all the gaps in consciousness. On the other hand, there may come a realization that this deeper sense of identity is not solid in itself, but is based in participation, the melting of distinctions. This is symbolized by the allegory of thinking of the nadir of the chart as pointing toward the earth's molten center, where all disparate elements are fused together. Here we see the fourth house's connection to the collective unconscious, to the whole of life, and participation in it through common myth.

However, we should recognize that the security most comfortable to ego is insular, not participatory. The symbology of universality of the fourth house is markedly uncomfortable to ego. That one's "true identity" is found by being actually at one with all others is contrary to being separate and distinct, except as mass consciousness serves to support one's illusions of distinction. (This challenge between first house separateness and fourth house universality is symbolized by the square between ascendant and nadir in the natural chart.) This may sound contradictory, but if we consider our experience, we may see that mass consciousness fosters a curious illusion of individuality. All of this is fourth-house (Moon-ruled) symbolism, and the connecting thread is depth of feeling, of being surrounded by the comfort of emotion and habit patterns. On one level, it is protection, the safety of the past; on the other, it can be exposure to its depths. (The fourth house is explored more fully in Chapters Six and Seven.)

These two levels suggest that each house (or sign or planet) may be interpreted dually, according to what we might call its "higher" and "lower" manifestations. This parallels the Buddhist notion that each form of ego-clinging or ignorance has its parallel in enlightenment. The level at which a person operates may be indicated astrologically by how much he remains fixed at one point in the symbolic cycle, refusing to accept the natural flux of experience, the truth of impermanence. For example, the security of participating in a deeper sense of wholeness that goes beyond the self is of itself an acceptance of change and flux. At each point in the cycle, one must let go in order to reveal its enlightenment potential, experiencing that stage fully without clinging.

Once ego has found its imagined security, the next stage is personal creativity. One traditional version of this moves from the security of the home (fourth house) to create children (fifth house). More generally, from an inner sense of identity, one creates; or, on another level, true creativity gives voice to the collective, hidden energies generated in the fourth house. It may also give voice to the intimate details of one's locale, but true art has a universal aspect, combining the "home" and "collective unconscious" levels of fourth-house experience as expressed through the fifth. An example of the connection between the fourth house and the fifth is found in Herman Melville's horoscope, with its fourth-house Sun in Leo and a fifth-house Mercury. Melville gave voice to hidden, unconscious drives and energies, symbolized by a great white whale (Moby Dick) and other powerful, numinous symbols. Melville produced his finest work when his home environment was secure and nurturing. (The collective nature of Melville's horoscope is indicated by a fourth-house Sun and other factors.)

The sixth house furnishes situations which may cause one to rethink the relationship between inner identity and personal creativity, as well as to refocus one's energy toward useful ends. Traditionally associated with work and service, the sixth house also symbolizes a process of learning and discovering that (though personal creativity may express inner identity or collective energies) is not an end in itself, no matter how bright its light. The sixth house is therefore a stage of psychological readjustment, crucial to the transformative process being described. In the fifth house, ego is seen in creative output that seems natural to it; the sixth house adjustment is to demands from beyond the personal realm: the need to work, or to find a social function for one's creations, to adjust creatively to others. In this house adjustment is needed to relate one's personal creativity to a social function through active and equal relationship with others. Social function and equality are symbolized by the seventh house; the sixth indicating inequality, learning (in which inequality may be a teacher) and reexamination (ruled by Mercury).

In the seventh house, the cycle of outreach emerges into the external realm in its primary emphasis. The first six houses incubate the energy of outreach before it can be fully externalized to make contact with other energies. The sixth house perfects this outreach by teaching how to readjust and grow through contact with others; the seventh emphasizes true relationship on an equal basis.

In the seventh house, ego finds and supports itself through one-on-one relationships. This is often a more fragile and shifting kind of support than the security of the home, or the solidity of values, or even temperament. Ego extends itself beyond fifth-house creativity and then undergoes sixth-house adjustments in order to expand more fully (because from ego's point of view that is the purpose of sixth-house learning). In this process, ego finds that its own expansion results in a marked change of focus: the need to recognize and deal with others. The final six houses show how continued outreach can become more and more enmeshed in external involvements, just as the first six show how it can become more and more involved in internal involvements; in both cases the final house of the group provides an opportunity to let go. In the sixth house, this opportunity comes through offering one's creative light to others. The final six houses show an even more clear potential for liberation, as the continued outreach can loosen ego's hold on its initial reference point of separation. Ego can either see its own game as empty or become imprisoned by its own extension.

The eighth house is a crucial stage in this process. Due to the values that result from relationship, ego undergoes a marked transformation. There should come a realization that true relatedness necessitates that one give up emotional territory, or in some sense "die to oneself." This is aptly symbolized by the loss of self in love-making, the "little death" of medieval terminology; but such loss is itself a symbol of a more pervasive truth: that true coming-togetherness requires giving up oneself. The eighth house symbolizes one's participation in experiences that bring this about (whereas Scorpio is more the archetypal energy itself).

The second and eighth houses are crucial to the potential for liberation symbolized in the two hemispheres (and by the entire cycle of the houses). They each provide values necessary for the experiential sequence symbolized by the houses which liberate and not imprison. If second-house values are materialistic, then the third house becomes an immediate environment resulting from those values, and the fourth house home becomes insular, protecting what is owned. From there, fifth-house creations give off not universal light, but the arrogance of an isolated ego. The sixth house may then be seen as a necessary evil instead of an opportunity to serve others or to learn techniques of purification, the purifying of ego's self-concern. If eighth-house values are materialistic, then the power generated becomes that of the ninth house—expansive and conquering. If, on the other hand, eighth-house values concern the need to die to oneself, then the ninth house becomes an opportunity to develop a sense of meaning and purpose from the death of the ego unto itself.

The ninth house indicates, on one hand, the experience of an expanded view of the world which comes when one incorporates the values of others. On the other hand, it is a house of learning—or the experiences of learning—and being a "fire-sign house,"* acts on the learning which has resulted from the death and rebirth energy release of the eighth house. If one experiences and accepts eighth-house pervasiveness and depth of change, the ninth-house experience can be truly expansive in a spiritual way. If one resists this change, the expansions of the ninth enhance ambition. But in any case, the extremely emotional experiences of the eighth house need to be seen in perspective; one needs to make sense of them.

Thus, the ninth house is religious insofar as religion promulgates a body of knowledge which "makes sense" of the death and rebirth process, of the fact that all things pass away and that birth requires death. Christianity holds such truths in the death and resurrection of Jesus the Christ, in the Gospels, and in the visions of Paul, who wrote of the need to die and be born again in Christ. Buddhism teaches about the death of ego and the rebirth into compassion, openness, and working for others.

From the expansiveness of the ninth house, ego extends in-

---

*See the glossary for an explanation of the elements of fire, earth, water, and air.

to the field of public position and honor, thereby giving tangible forms to its expansion. In the tenth, ego attempts to solidify through tangible reward and social position. For those who have accepted the dying of the eighth house, the tenth becomes one of mission and vocation. From the negative manifestations of the eighth—the tenth might become a career resulting from the expansive use of others' money. The hope of the tenth house is that in either case ego is rapidly expanding beyond any territory it can control; the remark of Jesus about gaining the world and losing one's soul often touches a respondent chord in even the most hardened tycoon. The issue is whether one is trying to "gain the whole world" or give oneself to it via a sense of mission or vocation.

Mahatma Gandhi's horoscope stands as an example of optimum tenth-house expression: a tenth-house Leo Moon trine to both a sixth-house Neptune and a second-house Saturn.* Situations abounded in which Gandhi was a central, shining public figure in compassionate service which dealt with issues of value and necessity. The Moon's position indicates his powerful public influence; the trines the potential for positive creative response. Neptune and Saturn point to the coming together, in his vocation, of practicality and illumination. A less fortunate use of similar energy is exemplified by the horoscope of Hitler, which has Saturn in Leo in the tenth house. As with Gandhi, the Leonine and Saturnian energies combined, but produced markedly different modes of expression.

The eleventh house maps the further extension of outreach into social networks. If ego has, in the tenth house, insisted on holding to career and reputation as support (if one is, like Shakespeare's Hotspur in *Henry IV*, pursuing that "bubble, reputation"), then the eleventh house may indicate either loss of control of that insistence or enhance its further expansion. If one has experienced the tenth house through selfless vocation, the eleventh house is a place where such public work networks through society, or through associates, so that ego's self-importance (which may remain even in altruistic vocations) becomes less and less centralized. On another level, ego

---

*See the glossary under "Aspects" for an explanation of trine.

may see that its creations come through groups, not simply from its own central reference point (i.e., fifth-house/eleventh-house polarity). One can realize here that one's vocation must lead to a true brotherhood of man.

Finally, in the twelfth house ego can come to realize that if it holds to any stake in its own creation, even at the eleventh-house stage of social betterment, it becomes bound and imprisoned in that world of associates, friends, and networks that result from retaining a subtle sense of self-reference. On the other hand, one can also come to realize that after fully extending oneself to encompass the "brotherhood of man," one is in an appropriate position to go further, to let go of any remaining fixation. Examples of twelfth house manifestation on two levels are: the businessman whose vision is blocked not only by ambition (tenth house), but also by the world of associates and empty hopes that are so closely connected to it (eleventh house); the server of humanity who realizes fully that the only logical extension of his vocation dedicated to the brotherhood of man is to give up the imprisoning hold on personal identity that is preventing his full participation and empathy.

Thus the twelfth house can be a prison due to ignorance, or the willing imprisonment of selfless giving where one allows oneself to be bound by the needs of others. From another point of view, the twelfth can be a house of an innocent, fresh perception of the world, of a clarity that is like the hours just after dawn, for the twelfth is the house into which the Sun rises, indicating a time which is not yet sullied or complicated by our desires. The connection between the dawn manifestation and the prison manifestation is that the twelfth house is an area of letting go, of accepting things without judgment (that is, letting go of judgment based on desire to be separate or to fulfill separative desires). With the dropping of judgment and desire, we can see our experience clearly. One level of this is seeing the dawn-freshness of the world. Another is seeing into our subconscious mind, the source of our imprisonment, which can be seen two ways: that which results from our separative outreach, or that of subconscious mind which impels us, without examination, into the next cycle with increased insistence on our power. The twelfth house may also be viewed as learning that one's vocation (tenth house) and creativity through others (eleventh) lead logically and experientially to realization that one needs to work from a selfless basis. If this learning is resisted, one is imprisoned by the resultant ignorance, the karma of the next cycle of ego-driven outreach, whether it be the next project, the next thought-chain, or the next lifetime.

In other words, there comes a point when one is imprisoned by the simple notion that one has done anything at all, or can, or that one is separate and free in the first place (first house). Traditionally the house of karma, the twelfth, symbolizes those areas of inner, outer, and social experience through which one can let go of one's self-insistence long enough to see the karmic chain more clearly. The twelfth may be seen as a house of spiritual demand or obligation: one must admit one's powerlessness and be empowered by it. As the house of the subconscious mind, the last house exerts a hidden control which undermines any attempt to act on the basis of a selflessness that only pretends to be complete.

As the end of the entire cycle, the twelfth indicates a final readjustment in preparation for a new cycle of outreach, and optimally the new cycle will be energized by the knowledge that one is powerless as a separate ego; for isolation leads inevitably to imprisonment. At the same time, however, separation can lead to liberation, and in fact the whole notion of liberation cannot exist apart from separation. Without ignorance, there is no enlightenment. The cycle of houses demonstrates, above all, the stage of ego's attempts to create for itself a solid world.

The argument that the twelve houses symbolize a series of stages in ego-transformation is not the traditional one. In the end, however, the issue is not whether astrological tradition agrees with such an interpretation—and it may not, for Western astrology has passed through cultures which basically accept the validity of ego and its potency. The point at issue is whether experience unfolds in this way, whether we can find a path, in our outreach into the various experiences that unfold in our lives, that leads to release and liberation. While we may agree that the planets contain liberation in their symbolism (i.e., that human psychology has certain transformational powers), or that the signs symbolize a spiritualizing process (i.e., that the archetypal pattern is a liberating one), we may have trouble accepting that the process of liberation or spiritualization is found right within our mundane and extremely personal experience or approach to life, that it may be found by attentively following the natural outreach of our individual temperament. In the cycle of the houses, the process of transformation is "brought down to earth" and becomes extremely personal, applying directly to the intimate details of our lives. Where the planets show that ego's central reference point is meant to be transformed psychologically, and the signs show the basic nature of energy transformation, the houses show us how the pattern of transformation becomes a personal path for each of us.

Reversing the Wheel

The logic of following the houses numerically, and thus following the parallel between the signs and houses, might be said to follow the logic of the mind. This is because the signs are basically man's projections into the heavens of his own seasonal and developmental round. As shown, such logic, based on simple survival, contains the seeds of liberation. These seeds are found at every point in the cycle, symbolizing the fact that liberation and spiritual growth are open to us at all times, in all experiences; we merely have to wake up to what is present. In addition, there are certain more persuasive points—stages where one's development or experience seems fairly to demand a new perspective on life. Generally this means less ego-involvement.

The numerical logic of the houses seems to be the logic of human outreach. Curiously, however, it is not the logic of the Sun, which rises into the twelfth house, reaches the midheaven approximately at noon, the descendant at sundown, and the nadir at midnight. If the numerical order is that of reflecting ego's projections, what is the order from twelve to one?

It is the order of the Sun. On one level, it may be the order of one's arrogance. In that case, rising into the twelfth, arrogance is tenuous so that one seeks friends and associates and from that tries to achieve something in the world. Career results from basic insecurity and tenuousness, not because the insubstantiality is negative in itself, but because one resists its truth. The show of arrogance becomes greater even as it feels less solid.

This sequence may be viewed another way, however (noting that either the numerical ordering or this one has "higher" and "lower" manifestations). If one emerges into the world and feels tenuous, one may accept the fragile beauty of such a situation as one accepts and appreciates the fragile beauty of the dew in the sunrise. In other words, one may accept the tenuousness of one's outreach, symbolized by the twelfth house. This also acknowledges that initial outreach is into the prison house of the world.

From this starting point, we may briefly describe the reversed cycle of the houses as follows: Because one accepts the essential tentativeness and groundlessness of outreach and experience (twelfth house), one engages in an idealized community or brotherhood—idealized because it is groundless (eleventh). From this relationship with others, one engages in some kind of work in the world (tenth) which expands one's vision (ninth). This naturally enables one to see the pervasiveness of death and change in the world (eighth), and this becomes the basis not only for balance but also for relationship (seventh). Relatedness, from a selfless perspective, demands that one serve or be a "servant of servants" (sixth), which is actually the basis of true creation and full creativity because it stems from nonarrogance (fifth). (On another level, creativity results from purity of applied technique.) This full creativity lights up the depths (fourth) and is the basis of tangible community, or a community which has depth (third) and leads to fruitful values and the valuing (second) of the isolated individual's need to sacrifice himself toward a greater whole (first and twelfth again).

This is a direction that does not easily support ego, because it begins tentatively, though it can be perverted if one looks away from tentativeness and groundlessness, and if one refuses to confront one's fear. That willingness to confront one's fear —which means also looking into one's subconscious mind— and the willingness to become immersed in the fragile, tender beauty of the world is the basis for reversing the wheel of karma.

The twelfth house appears, on the one hand, as the repository of our repression, our "repressed or unacknowledged self"[7] that must be integrated with the conscious self. Robert Hand, contemporary astrologer, calls twelfth-house energy "the individual's first tentative attempts to put something out into the world."[8] As such, he continues, it is easily defeated, and thus repressed. In this way, our unacknowledged fears become the true "hidden enemies" of the twelfth, and it is these we must confront, first and last, if we are to engage ourselves in any spiritual path.

For this reason, the twelfth not only represents hidden enemies and the subconscious mind, but also monasteries and places of retreat. On one level, we might say that monastics invite repression by society-at-large because society cannot incorporate them into the mainstream since they represent an unwordly orientation that is opposed to the self-definition of most societies. On another level, a monastery is a place where one confronts the unconscious mind directly. Monasticism is obviously not required to do this, but the principle is clear: we must look into our repressions, not only through meditation or contemplation, but through looking into our tentativeness, our doubts, and, through accepting feedback from the world, into those facets of ourselves which others see, but which we do not.

Finally, as the house of the hours just past dawn, the twelfth is the house of the world's tentativeness, its fragile beauty. It is strange that we are ready to accept the beauty of early morning, yet hide our own fragility. But it is here in inner and outer sensitivity and openness, that we are strongly induced to drop those attachments that drive karma onward. And it is our fear of our own fragility that prevents us from seeing the fragility of the world, the basis for compassion.

A Complete Picture

It is said in the Buddhist teachings that if there were no samsara—the round of ignorance and delusion driven by the grasping of ego—then there would be no nirvana or enlightenment. This idea is also borne out in astrological symbolism, both through the different levels at which each symbol may be interpreted, and through the movements of the groups of symbols which have just been outlined and the ways the process of ego-grasping can be naturally transformed into liberation.

The groups of symbols have been described as stages in a process, and it is sometimes the popular notion that the later stages, or outermost planets, are more spiritual than the earlier ones. For example, Pisces is often considered to be a highly spiritual sign, whereas Aries is considered self-centered. We need to realize that Pisces and Aries are part of the same process, the same cyclic development. Without Aries there is no Pisces, and the symbolic meaning of Pisces is inseparable from that of Aries. Similarly, Neptune and Pluto are part of the same planetary system as Mars and are presumably part of the same gravitational field. So, on a physical level, the movement of one planet is inseparable from that of another.

Our dualistic judgments, here as elsewhere, can become problematic. The issue is a complete picture of man. Without a full understanding of what we are, it is senseless to speak of spirituality in any useful way. On another level, we have seen that even the supposedly malefic energies have important spiritual uses. For example, Martian one-pointedness is a technique which forms part of spiritual practice; Saturn can indicate the need to apply some form of discipline. Neptune, so often called the planet of enlightenment, can indicate obfuscation and overidealization that is detrimental to spiritual growth. Similarly, the ascendant and first house can indicate the physical structure and separation of the person who engages in spiritual practice in the first place. We need to remind ourselves, as the Buddha reminded his followers, that there is no such thing as an unsuitable candidate.

It is pointless to speak of "spiritual growth" apart from our own experience, and that experience is symbolized through the entire body of astrological symbolism. It does not make sense to make value judgments about which levels of the symbolic processes are more spiritual than others, especially if by these judgments we ignore the cyclic nature of our experience and the way all facets of life are interdependent. From the standpoint of spiritual growth, we are simply caught on the wheel; and we may be caught as easily by our notions of spirituality as by our drive for social or personal distinction.

Seen another way, the statement that there is no nirvana without samsara is reflected in each individual symbol. The outgoing and ingoing movements of the planetary system demonstrate that each planet has an enlightened and an ignorant usage. The same is true for the signs and houses. Pisces can be either self-sacrifice, based on an egoless perspective, or loss of will in the blind chaos of mass delusion. Taurus can be either sensuality without perspective or an immovability based on firm value, leading to wisdom (as symbolized by the Buddha himself, said to have been born on a full moon in May). Scorpio can be either brutal power or essential transformation. Capricorn can be either blind ambition or the determined climb to the heights of clarity, mission, and rock-like wisdom based on experience.

The need to see beyond the polarities of "good" and "bad" facets of astrological symbols is essential if we are to see the system as a whole. This statement, applied here particularly to astrology, is merely a restatement of the more general truth that we must see through the judgments with which we overlay our experience: for our judgments are our personal way of seeing the world in terms of polarities. The need to do otherwise is clearly stated by the late W.Y. Evans-Wentz, in his introduction to *The Tibetan Book of the Great Liberation:*

> Tantricism, in its higher esoteric reaches, of which Europeans have but little knowledge, propounds, as do all philosophies, ancient and modern, based upon the occult sciences, that the ultimate truth (at least from the viewpoint of man) is neither this nor that, neither *Sangsara* nor *Nirvana*, but at-one-ment, wherein there is transcendence over all opposites, over both good and evil.[9]

5

The Outer Planets and Collective Projection

In the previous chapter the three major symbol systems of astrology were explained from the standpoint of the development of ego and man's spiritual potential that demands that he grow beyond ego's confines. The planets were described as components of man's psychological makeup, as a group of psychological energies. Their interconnections demonstrate the process of ego development followed by the breakdown of ego so that spiritual growth can take place. The emphasis was primarily internal: man as man, without necessary reference to the external world. The signs were described as a process of energy development which may be seen in the seasons or in other processes of growth, fruition, and withdrawal. The houses were described in terms of tangible, usually social, outreach. The signs and houses were generally referred to the external world more than were the planets.

One question that may arise from those descriptions is why the three systems are not parallel. In particular, why is the psychological process symbolized by the planets not parallel to the archetypal pattern symbolized through the signs or the experiential pattern symbolized through the houses? Why should the psychological process differ from the organic one?

If the human psyche is part of the same reality as nature, why should the planetary pattern (the psyche) not parallel the patterning of the organic world (the signs)?

The Buddhist teachings say that ego drives samsara (the cycle of birth, death, and illusion-delusion). This is reflected in the astrological use of planetary rulerships for the signs: the psychological energies which make up ego are related to the signs which connect to the organic round of birth, growth, flowering, decay, and finally rebirth.

In traditional astrology, there was a clear parallel between these two sets of symbols. Each planet is ruled by two signs, its "day" sign and its "night" sign; the Sun and the Moon ruled one sign each. Therefore, if one begins with Cancer and Leo, ruled by the Moon and Sun respectively, and moves in either direction, one follows, via the rulerships, the same pattern described in the previous chapter. The following table shows this ordering:

Leo	Sun	Cancer	Moon
Virgo	Mercury	Gemini	Mercury
Libra	Venus	Taurus	Venus
Scorpio	Mars	Aries	Mars
Sagittarius	Jupiter	Pisces	Jupiter
Capricorn	Saturn	Aquarius	Saturn

This ordering includes only the planets out to and including Saturn. In either direction, one goes through the process of ego outreach and solidification, out to the crystallization symbolized by Saturn. Then one returns to the center. The energy of return is that of Saturn: the crystallization and bureaucratization of ego.

Pictured here is the projection of an orderly, stable society and world. The point is not that all was peaceful, but that the changes that took place were all within the bounds defined by Saturn. Wars replaced one Saturnian structure with another; they did not threaten mass death or complete annihilation. That the world was not considered perfect is indicated by Saturn's designation as the "greater malefic." We might also say that the world was ruled by the individual shadow, or the limited definition of man, resulting from insecurity and fear which had been cemented into the social structure.

In short, what we see in this perfect alignment of the planets and signs is a stable world in which there was no collective knowledge about the country beyond ego. Though stable, the world was strongly delimited.

With the discovery of the three outer planets, the orderly arrangement between signs and planets broke down. Parallel to this, the world order—or the relation between man and his world—became similarly skewed. Man is no longer in a static harmony with his world but in a relationship of dynamic tension, of disharmony seeking reharmonization. We might call it a period of potentially creative chaos.

The reader is requested, in the following discussion, not to assume that I reject the older rulers. This is certainly not true on a practical level, as in application Mars still seems to hold some rulership over Scorpio, and Venus over Taurus. When I suggest, further on, that Chiron be considered as an appropriate ruler for Virgo, I do not mean to deny the ordinary connection of Mercury to Virgo. These proposed new rulers may be seen as deepening our understanding of a sign, not doing away with the significance of previous rulers. The point is that newly discovered planets "skew" the planet-sign relationship; or, we may say that Uranus did so, true to its nature, while all subsequent discoveries are part of the path toward a new balancing.

If we take only the newest rulers for each sign, we have the following order:

Leo . . . . Sun	Cancer . . . . Moon
Virgo . . . . Mercury	Gemini . . . . Mercury
Libra . . . . Venus	Taurus . . . . Venus
Scorpio . . . . Pluto	Aries . . . . Mars
Sagittarius . . . . . . Jupiter	Pisces . . . . Neptune
Capricorn . . . . Saturn	Aquarius . . . . Uranus

One way of describing this confusion is to say that human psychology is out of line with the archetypal and organic pattern of growth and decay, or out of phase with its world. On one hand, this is evident; man *is* out of harmony with his

world—dismayingly so. This is true insofar as we compare
the present to the past; but there may be a more hopeful way
to look at the situation. The symbolism of the planets implies
that ego is meant to be transformed because man has within
him the transformative energies symbolized by Uranus, Neptune, and Pluto. Transformation, by definition, moves away
from stasis and the status quo. We need to look at this skewed
relationship more closely. It indicates instability, but what
is its inner nature?

Various writers (e.g., Liz Green, Jungian analyst and
astrologer, and Dane Rudhyar) have suggested that the discovery of new planets symbolizes new stages in the potential
for conscious spiritual growth; such growth stages become
available to mankind collectively. (The signs, on the other
hand, are a closed system. There are unlikely to be any newly discovered signs.) The new planets indicate that humanity
is in a period of imbalance based on seeing that consciousness
is distinct from the ongoing round of birth and death. Because
of this, one can come to an objective perspective on that
round. The development of consciousness beyond ego (symbolized by the trans-Saturnian planets) indicates that one can
break from the circle of karma and samsara, the wheel on
which ego is bound.

Those readers familiar with the Tibetan iconography of the
"wheel of life" will recognize parallels here. The Buddha
stands outside of the wheel. The wheel represents the entire
round of birth and death and the various fantasies which give
it life and sustain it. The wheel is held by a demon, and the
Buddha stands outside the wheel, pointing the way to enlightenment. Similarly, consciousness, symbolized by the planets,
can potentially stand outside the wheel of life symbolized by
the houses and signs; yet, via the planetary rulerships, consciousness can still exert influence on that realm, hopefully
toward the creation of an enlightened society, one not based
on ego.

It is worth noting, however, that consciousness standing
outside the realm of birth and death does not mean death is

overcome or that the body is immortal. In the horoscope, the body is ruled largely by the ascendant, which is part of the wheel. The separation of planets and signs, introduced by newly discovered planets, does not obviate the significance of the signs or houses, but merely indicates that human consciousness is not necessarily completely involved in, or defined through, the cycle of birth and death (or the hope and fear that seems so inseparable from them). So the chaos is hopeful.

As noted, the discovery of new planets seems to coincide with the potentiality of significant forward steps in the development of human consciousness on a mass scale. It is as if the universe, or Greater Whole, is saying to mankind, "Here is an energy which you now need to cope with. The time has come for you to understand this type of energy, and it is therefore being introduced into your world. It is available for all of you to understand, and in fact it is necessary that you understand it."

We might call these new discoveries new demands in our evolution, indications that it is time for us to take the next step. The catch is that it is not possible to stay where we are. In Yeats' words, "a terrible beauty is born." We can either work with the energy consciously, as a factor in personal transformation (which the ego will, of course, resist), or repress the energy and experience it in a more difficult form as a projection into the collective realm.

Projection is a concept usually associated with personal psychology. It may be defined as an ego-defense mechanism in which an individual attributes unacceptable desires and impulses to others.[1] Recalling our personal projections—or seeing through them—is essential in any effort toward personal growth, an issue underscored by Jung in his writings on the shadow, the anima, and the animus.[2] Liz Greene, who has related astrological concepts to Jungian ideas, describes projection this way:

> When a person projects some unconscious quality existent within himself onto another person, he reacts to the projec-

tion as though it belongs to another; it does not occur to
him to look within his own psyche for the source of it . . . .
This very simple mechanism is at work whenever we have
any highly colored or irrational emotional reaction, positive
or negative, to another person.[3]

In the present work, projections are seen in terms of astrological symbolism, and may be roughly divided into two types:
personal and collective. Personal planets, those within
Uranus's orbit, tend to "come at us" in a negative or difficult
form when projected; but the projection is personal and usually has no collective significance. The outer planets, however,
are collective and impersonal by nature; so our response to
them must be of a different nature. Response to personal planets is simply a matter of integrating personality factors:
response to the outer planets involves integrating those energies
that break down our sense of who we are. On another level,
overcoming projection is owning, without self-blame, our intimate bond with the destructiveness we see in our world, because when the collective response to the transformative
energies of Uranus, Neptune, and Pluto is simply to repress
them, their energies emerge as a collective projection.

In general, we project onto others that which we devalue
and reject in ourselves. This is particularly the case with the
outer planets because, as energies which transform the ego,
they are quite likely to be rejected or devalued by that ego.
This, combined with the collective nature of the outer planets, indicates that the collective manifestations of those outer
planets are actually the same as our own potentials for transformation. We need to deal with these energies one way or
another. Apparently we may do this in two ways: We may
try to incorporate them into a conscious path of ego-tran-
scendence or we may experience them in the form of collective energies. As collective energies they are difficult to deal
with because the conscious ego has devalued them at the
source of projection.

The coincidence of the planetary discoveries with new
sociological and political developments that lead to greater
collectivity suggests that the new developments, however difficult, are in some way appropriate or necessary. The new
planets were, after all, "waiting to be discovered."

The instability that has resulted, both in human consciousness and in the phenomenal world, demands growth and transformation, development and transition. The challenges that are brought forth are not to be ignored nor relegated to the realm of already understood undesirable elements. There will be challenges to humanity that upset our collective balance and force us to grow beyond old paradigms. But the problem lies in our response to such challenges, which is so often based on old assumptions about the nature of man and the purpose of life.

These assumptions are symbolized by the traditional seven planets: Sun, Moon, Mercury, Venus, Mars, Jupiter, and Saturn. Saturn, the outermost, symbolizes the bureaucracy and structured defense mechanism of ego or of its reflection, the nation state, kingdom, or whatever is being defended. The discovery of Uranus, and subsequently of Neptune, Pluto, and finally the planetoid, Chiron, implies not only an instability that upsets the psychological and planetary status quo, but also an instability in which the only workable response is one from beyond the realm of ego.

Any solution must fit the problem, and the problem here is defined by the symbolism of the outer three planets and by their effects on the status quo in the astrological system itself (the skewed relationship); in human psychology (the unbalanced feeling present in so many people); and in the social-collective order (the present world situation). So we should seek our solution through the symbolism of these same three planets. (Chiron is important here as well, and will be discussed; but it is not of the same nature as the other three, being defined as a "planetoid," possibly not originally part of the solar system. It is important as a catalyst for solution, but is not so clearly reflected as an aspect of the collective.)

In other words, we will not solve the problems facing us by referring back to an old order in which ego rules, or in which decisions are made based on the assumption that our world is full of egos which can potentially be satisfied if only we structure (Saturn) things properly. Saturn is the symbol of this search for structure on a psychological level. On a worldwide basis it becomes the search resulting from an unconsidered (Saturn as individual Shadow) assumption about the solidity (Saturn) of ego based on optimism and learning (Jupiter), aggression (Mars), love and beauty (Venus), thinking and communication (Mercury), emotional habit patterns and security needs (Moon), and a sense of creative, central reference point, or simple arrogance (Sun). Solutions to personal or collective malaise will simply be ineffective if they work from such a paradigm. New wine bursts through old skins, as the world situation indicates quite clearly.

New solutions or directions must come from the logic of new discoveries—new as far as collective, conscious knowledge is concerned. The three other planets are transcendental because they exceed the limitations of an ego-bound point of view. Socially or psychologically, ego cannot control these energies. As Liz Greene remarks, "You can always try controlling a transit of Uranus, Neptune, or Pluto, but I wish you luck."[4] The new wine of collective experience is currently bursting the old skins in dangerous ways—ways which with Pluto moving through the sign of Scorpio may be quite dangerous to human survival. *

The new skins to contain this wine, enabling all to drink, must be made from the knowledge (and resulting praxis) that ego is not something meant to endure, not some solid reference point, but is meant to be transformed. The products of the forces of disintegration around us and the ongoing threat of calamity to the world itself may be seen as projections of our need for inner transformation. When we ignore this need, we experience the transformative energies of the outer three planets as projections in the environment. As such, they often "come at us" in their negative form.

There is a message in the process of destruction: something *has* to die. If insight (Uranus) doesn't shatter our various presumptions about solidity, and if we don't allow these presumptions to dissolve as a result of greater vision (Neptune), then the next step is destruction or death (Pluto). The threat we perceive to the world is parallel to—and actually inseparable from—the demanded breakdown and transformation of ego's complex, insecure, trickster-like kingdom. Strange and escapist

*Pluto transits the sign of Scorpio from 1984 until 1995.

as it may sound, the astrological symbolism implies that the solution to the world's problems lies in the same area as the threat itself: in the human heart and consciousness. The solution is in an emptiness of the heart, the emptiness of ego-devastation indicated by Pluto. This leads to a transformed view of our personal Sun or creative source, atomically powered like the bomb and able to transform the earth. In Jungian terminology, we must recall our projections to ourselves, which in this case, following the astrological symbolism, means personal transformation through the threefold process symbolized by Uranus, Neptune, and Pluto (and, as will be explained, Chiron). As projections, these appear respectively as high technology, mass emotionalism or mass deception, and concentrated power related to concentrated wealth and the power to deal out destruction.

Uranus: Sudden Insights

As an image of personal transformation, Uranus is sudden insight, the flash that illuminates the landscape of ego, giving light so that one becomes aware of greater space beyond and above ego's limited, plotted-out territory. We could call Uranus a bringer of "creative space." It is the opening that allows important new ideas to come forth—the idea that there *is* something more than ego. But Uranus does not tell us what to do with that space, and its flash of insight is so sudden that the ego cannot grasp and hold it as ego would like. So to ego this space is threatening.:

> People are afraid of the emptiness of space, or the absence of company, the absence of a shadow . . . . It is generally a fear of space, a fear that we will not be able to anchor ourselves to any solid ground, that we will lose our identity as a fixed and solid and definite thing. This could be very threatening.[5]

Space is creative simply because there's nothing there. If there is no space, there is no room for creation. If the flash symbolized by Uranus did more than simply break through ego's walls to provide space—if it tried to do something to fill that space—then the space could not properly be called "creative." Therefore, the very fact that Uranus provides space is the reason for its seeming threat (to ego) and also its promise. If space is filled with preconceived ideas, it becomes ego's realm, Saturn-Satan operating as trickster, no longer space at all.

The insecurity one feels with Uranus is essential to the transformative process. Ego is suddenly presented with a lightning-like insight that there is something (like lightning) that it can't control. The idea dawns that its cherished realm—astrologically symbolized by the limit of Saturn—is not at all the whole picture. (We might say facetiously that Saturn "isn't the whole ball game," and is more like the umpires, who can feel threatened if the game generates too much energy.)

Mythologically, Uranus is a sky god and father to Saturn who castrated him. The indication here is that insight preceded ego; space preceded restriction. But the myth suggests that ego sees its purpose as taking away the creative or fecundating power of space or insight (which is, on one level, awareness of space). This aspect of the myth seems to be reflected in Uranus's somewhat asexual nature: its energy is fecundating, but through ideas (or Idea) instead of sexuality.

On a social level, Uranus rules high technology, networking, electronic transfer of information, and in general the technical or communicative aspect of the "global village." It is also the new idea, particularly that of freedom.[6] From the standpoint of ego trying to establish its place in the world (Saturn), freedom is simply latitude (Chapter Eight). From the standpoint of Uranus, real freedom is from the bounds of ego, but because Uranus functions unconsciously in most people, and without their objective understanding, attempts to break out of Saturnian patterns remain mostly social in their consequences. It becomes a sort of compulsive breaking away, not for any spiritual purpose but simply in response to a feeling of restriction.

Socially, Uranus may also manifest as an entrance into a sense of brotherhood or involvement in some sort of "group

consciousness," but again, unless Uranian insight has illumi-
nated the real limitation of ego-bound consciousness and activity, such involvement will not lead to true spiritual growth.
However, insofar as Uranus *does* break apart those social
attachments which ego uses to steady and secure itself (as
much as possible), its energies can bring a fruitful panic. Seeing ego without its usual supports can itself be insightful.

Uranus was discovered in 1781 by William Herschel, an
English astronomer. Writers have pointed out that that year
coincided with the promulgation of ideas such as individual
liberty and freedom and their emergence through Saturnian
boundaries via the American and French Revolutions. Perhaps even more important was the translation into English
and German of a number of Sanskrit scriptures, thus bringing to the West the Eastern idea of spiritual traditions and
techniques that work with energies that go beyond the realm
of ego. (William Jones, known as "Oriental" Jones, was a
scholar of Asiatic literature who founded the Royal Asiatic
Society. Though his interest was primarily in Sanskrit texts,
he was also interested in Chinese and Tibetan culture.)[7]

The new ideals of freedom and liberty as promulgated
through the political ferment of that time were in some sense
coopted by the status quo: Saturn again castrated Uranus to
take away his life-giving power. Uranian energy in Saturnian
hands is still evident today, with technology in the service of
innumerable Saturnian corporations. The "control" of Uranus
by Saturn is still highly questionable, however, as the idea
of freedom quickly percolates through society. At the present
time, we see some high technology in the hands of artists who
seem anarchistic, as well as of actual anarchists. And the seeds
planted by the first translation of Oriental texts continue to
grow all over the Western world. It is important to remember
that the glyph for Uranus (♅) symbolizes growth of spirit
through matter to link the individual soul to the collective;
and in all its forms, however troublesome, Uranus attempts
to do this. The brotherhood of man—the linking of the two
soul-semicircles—is resulting from material and technological means.

The discovery of Uranus, in being coincident with the birth

of the American nation, is highly significant: America is not only a fertile ground for high technology, but also for the transplanted Eastern teachings which have taken root here. From a Buddhist perspective, this is no surprise, for there is a Buddhist prophecy that "when the iron bird flies and horses run on wheels, the Dharma [the Buddhist teachings] will go to the land of the Red Man."[8] So in one sense the "land of the free and the home of the brave" has become a place where those who are brave enough can strive to be free from ego.

On a psychological level, real freedom is deeply frightening. Ego resists it, as it always has. It therefore continues to build around itself such structures as will allow it to perpetuate the illusion. The Uranian need for a break with ego-bound consciousness is thus made unconscious, and as such it appears as a projection into the environment. One example of this is the way technology seems to run our lives: television antennas may indicate information leading to a global village, or they may indicate stupefication because of inundation with data. The ubiquity of these antennas—which look so much like Uranus' glyph—in our cities and towns may be seen as a projection of inner needs, emerging in negative form. The information we really need to receive is that we are not what we think we are.

This latter notion *is* becoming part of the consciousness of many, but the energy still seems primarily unconscious. The prevalence of Uranian symbolism indicates that information is available to us if we know what "channel" to tune to. It is simply a question of making the creative space conscious. All Uranian information moves through and announces this creative space; we need to see how we close off to it.

Neptune: Enlightenment/Delusion

The intelligent use of Neptune depends on the enlightened use of Uranus. The negative manifestation of these two energies working together is mass delusion (Neptune) depending on technology (Uranus). At the time of this writing, with Neptune in the sign of Capricorn,* this may be an overidealization of the past or of the status quo generally. With Uranus in the sign of Sagittarius,† we see a tremendous expansion of technology in many directions.

Another unfortunate manifestation of Neptune is widespread drug addiction, alcoholism, and simple mass emotionalism. All of these have a common denominator of submerging the ego—overcoming or inundating it through connection with something vaster, a yearning for the infinite or transcendant.

Neptune is also the planet of enlightenment, egoless self-sacrifice, and compassion. The manifestation of these depends on the initial insight of Uranus that sees the limits of ego. Without this understanding, compassion is not really just that, but another activity that aggrandizes the ego. But we should realize that both the alcoholic and the bodhisattva are yearning for (and with the bodhisattva actually working for) a situation in which individual egos are not separate.

Neptune, then, truly gives up the ego's hold. From this perspective, we see that pictures of Jesus on the Cross (sacrifice of ego to save others) and mass emotionalism, such as the fashion and entertainment industry, have the same principle in common: the individual ego confronts and is subjected to the energy of the whole. The difference is again in how much one is consciously aware of the demands of Neptune (and as noted, how one has first worked with the energies of Uranus). When Neptune is not made conscious, it is experienced as a projection, where its form is usually negative. Both Jesus and the addict give themselves up to the whole, but Jesus seems to have known exactly what he was doing, whereas the addict almost never seems to.

Because Neptune is not conscious in most people—a fact which we can see either by examination of individuals or by simply looking at the troubling Neptunian projections that pervade our world—special work on oneself is necessary to bring

---

*Neptune transits the sign of Capricorn from 1984 to 1998.

†Uranus transits the sign of Sagittarius from 1981 to 1988.

it to consciousness. In this regard, it is important to realize that making the energy conscious is not merely a matter of intellect. On one level, it would seem that everybody is conscious of the need for compassion: they know what the word means, surely, and will actually feel the energy in themselves, because it is in each of us. On another level, however, it is clear that people are not at all conscious of what Neptune—or true compassion—really demands. The issue is the sacrifice of a point of reference. We need to give up any hope of gain to realize Neptune fully. In some sense the statement, "I am a compassionate person," is never really true.

So when we say we need to make Neptune conscious, we mean that we need to realize Neptune fully in our lives. A "realized" person is called such not because he has an array of nice-sounding concepts, but because of what he has taken to heart. To really bring Neptune to conscious reality is to glimpse what selflessness really means in full experience, what it implies in terms of our cherished identity. It is not enough to talk about universal love like a messiah. Neptune demands hard experience, a broken heart in the face of the immense suffering of the world, and a willingness to give oneself up in compassionate action. This requires a glimpse or an insight into the limitations of the ego (Uranus); if this doesn't occur, Neptune becomes delusion, living in a dream world.

Neptune makes it easy to fool ourselves. It rules deception and tends to confuse true universal love and our idealized version of it. Its proper manifestation comes out of disciplined reality-testing—a hard look at the world, indicated by Saturn—resulting in the sudden Uranian insight that, because ego is essentially empty of inherent existence, it is possible to give birth to true compassion.

Instead, what we see around us is the mass of people who fill up their emptiness with emotion offered them by the status quo (Saturn) via technology (Uranus). The great sadness in this is that unconsciously the hearts of people *have* been emptied, but it is emptiness of a tragic sort. The technology of the status quo can also bring a vision of universal suffering, but the hypnotic power of technology (Uranus-Neptune connection) too often renders the viewer powerless. The result is that ego holds on to the reins as usual, pleads adherence to the status quo, and goes to work with everyone else on a Saturnian schedule, later to drown sorrows in drink and television.

Pluto: Concentrated Power

All of this might be merely tragic if it weren't for the energies symbolized by Pluto. Since the discovery of this last-known planet, the tragedy has become dangerous. Concentrated power and wealth moving the collective consciousness, resulting in mass emotion based on technology, and the full stability of the status quo precipitate an extremely potent situation, with the transformative energies in their projected, negative form. Instead of the transformation and devastation of ego, we are threatened with transformative destruction and devastation of the landscape of the world.

Pluto is potentially the complete repolarization of ego, its radical death. The god of the underworld is frightening and fertile, bringing both death and the potential for new, even transfigured life. When projected in its negative form, it becomes devastation resulting from hidden, concentrated power and wealth. In its positive, transformational form, it is a concentration and mobilization of power and individual resourcefulness from hidden reservoirs. This makes possible a true dying to old ways and a consequent refocalization and repolarization to the new.

Pluto is symbolic of a process in which a small amount of material, through a chain reaction, is able to bring about vast changes through a death-and-rebirth paradigm. This small amount of material may be plutonium, in the form of atomically fissionable bombs, or hydrogen in the form of fusion bombs; or it may be small, empowered groups of people who concentrate and focus energy on some transformative task. The key issue with Pluto is whether selflessness and compassion (Neptune) are the motivating factors. Pluto's energies in the service of ego are dangerous. The result seems to be the eruption on earth of the demonic forces of the underworld.

Pluto's energies in the service of compassion also result in the eruption of hidden forces, but in a more positive form. They still may not be completely pleasant, because ego will always resist its own death; but Uranian insight will show one their necessity. The point is that Pluto brings to the surface those deep-seated and even primitive drives and emotions which cannot be ignored in any spiritual work.

We may understand this better through a metaphor taken from the Buddhist tradition: It is said that the unskilled farmer throws away his manure and rubbish, while the skilled farmer collects his to spread on his garden.[9] The skilled farmer here has Uranian insight—sharp seeing through appearances to the true needs of the situation. This allows him to put the energies of Pluto, symbolized by manure (Pluto rules all waste products) to good use. The manure may be our emotions or situations of political power which seem to pollute or "lay waste to" the earth. It might be anything we wish would go away, but which contains within it the transformative power which comes from the acceptance of death and decay or breakdown. Pluto recognizes that "one's attitude towards death is central to any healing process."[10]

So again the issue is one of full, conscious acceptance (which will include acceptance of ego's resistance; the willingness to work with it). This in turn requires conscious acceptance and awareness of both Uranus and Neptune. It should also be noted that full and conscious acceptance is a commitment to the path. It does not mean that to deal with Pluto we must have fully accomplished the demands of Neptune. Commitment to integrate Uranus's insights and to live by selfless compassion leads logically and experientially to the repolarization experience of Pluto.

When Pluto serves the mass delusion projection of Neptune, we see situations on a small scale like the Jonestown, Guayana tragedy of 1979, or the incidents at Wounded Knee, South Dakota (1891), and on a larger scale the massive starvation reported in Cambodia in the late 1970s, and the spread of Nazi power in the 1930s; or even the proliferation of dictatorships based on global armament. When Pluto serves the selfless compassion of Neptune, we see situations such as Jesus dying on the Cross (leading to new life and transfiguration), Buddhism coming to America, the work of Mother Teresa and of Gandhi.

If we do not commit ourselves as a race to integrating these energies into ourselves, they will appear in the world as projections; and even if we *do* commit ourselves to the spiritual path, the strength of past karma and habit will result in our having to deal with projections anyway until those habits and karma are exhausted. Admittedly, that might be a long time. Nevertheless, we must begin somewhere. The astrological symbolism suggests that such a path is actually a pragmatic way to deal with the world situation as it now exists.

Pluto requires death of the ego and release of power, but it seems ego must consciously will its own transformation. That is, we might say on one level that the collective is composed of many egos which have in some sense died; died to their own full potential as human beings, preferring to rest in the delusions of Neptune provided by the technology of Uranus. In a more real sense, however, ego here seems actually reinforced by such delusion. The price for these reinforcements is the destructive manifestations of the outer planets on a collective scale. If ego seems to succeed in coopting the outer planetary energies, the price seems to be paid on a collective scale in the negative, projected form.

The importance of the difference between the collective and the transformational use of Uranus, Neptune, and Pluto is a more precise way of showing how man's spiritual development has not kept pace with his technological advancement. However, because of the multilayered symbolic meanings of the astrological symbols, they reveal to us a praxis, not merely a problem.

Some will argue that the energies of the transcendental planets *were* consciously recognized before the discovery of Uranus in 1781. In Buddhism, particularly in Japan and Tibet, there was a clear understanding of these energies and of their transformative character. Certainly the need to understand reality without ego pervaded Buddhism and seems implicit (if less concisely formulated in those terms) in Sufism and in early forms of Christianity. These teachings did not, as far as I know, relate these energies to planets, but saw them simply as part of the complete human being.

This does not contradict the notion that the discovery date of a planet marks the point at which the symbolized energy becomes part of human consciousness. In Tibet, though Buddhism was the state religion, the majority of the people did not relate to the teachings on the level of ego transformation. In any case, the awareness in Japan and Tibet in 1500 A.D. was clearly not at the collective level of the planet. Buddhism, Sufism, esoteric Christianity, and Western occultism generally were not part of the collective mentality. The energies of transcendence were latent in all men, as they are today, and the sages of earlier times were able to bring this latency to full conscious acceptance.

The pressing question for modern man is how to bring about this conscious acceptance. What is the method? Where does one begin? And how does one know, having once begun, that one has started out on a legitimate path? How does one guard against ego's constant tricksterism, by which even legitimate spiritual techniques can be poisoned?

Chiron: Bridging the Gap

As was suggested in the previous chapter, some of the answers to these questions are related to the symbolism of Chiron. The importance of Chiron in our present situation is indicated by its recent discovery; as noted already, the discovery of a new planet indicates a new stage of conscious growth available to collective humanity. Chiron can help us to make a fuller transformational use of the energies of the outer planets.

Mythologically, Chiron was the leader of the centaur race, known as the wisest of the centaurs, their priest-king. Half god, he was the offspring of Kronos and the nymph Philyra, who was changed into the form of a horse by Kronos, to evade Rhea, Kronos's jealous wife. As an adult, Chiron was a teacher

and sort of foster parent to many of the great warriors of
Greece, including Jason and Achilles. He was also teacher to
Asclepias, famed doctor and son of Apollo. Chiron taught the
arts of warriorship, hunting, healing, philosophy, prophecy,
music, and religion.[11]

Some astrologers have found the meaning of the planetoid
Chiron to parallel this mythological background. The planetoid has been found to be related to healing, to teaching and
to the symbols of key, bridge, foster parenting, catalyst. In
general, Chiron is thought to be a mediator or link between
Saturn and Uranus, or, in the terms we have been using so
far, between the realm of ego with its defenses (Saturn) and
the insight that breaks these defenses apart. It appears to be
associated with major changes in life direction; such a change
could obviously be away from allegiance to ego towards allegiance to the energies symbolized by the trans-Saturnian
planets.

In the second chapter, Chiron's symbolism was compared
to the traditional analogies for the guru in the Buddhist tradition. The point can be reiterated here, adding that the significance is not only one of personal, psychological growth,
but also involves our whole approach to the collective.

As well as the associations already mentioned, Chiron is
more specifically the energy which is needed to bridge the gap
between ego and non-ego, between Saturn's ego-bureaucracy
and the creative space of Uranus. Chiron's symbolism includes
those human figures who teach us how to do this, how to set
out on a trustworthy path which will enable us to bring the
powerful energies of the transcendental planets into our path
of personal transformation. On a true path we will guard
against the self-deception that is so much ego's stock in trade,
which would induce us to think that ego-serving activities are
really spiritual work. Put another way, Chiron's energy can
enable us to recall the negative, projected form of the trans-
Saturnians.

The importance of our recognition that we need such a
bridge, or need to recognize and accept such a teaching func-

tion, is indicated by how easily "spiritual" practices become perverted to worldly ends. In myth, Chiron lives in the mountains, and so stands apart from the Saturnian realm of worldly ambition, yet he is actually a son of Saturn. The implication seems to be that our ambition can give birth to that knowledge which can lead us beyond it. Chiron shows us, on the one hand, how to relate our animal nature (ruler of the wild centaur race) and our need to form civilized structures based on ambition. On the other hand, he shows us how to turn those ambitions, or even the insecure structure of ego itself, toward a spiritual purpose. As the son of Saturn, Chiron is the grandson of Uranus, and thus has both discipline and insight in his family lineage.

It is significant, too, that Chiron is not visible to the naked eye and not even readily visible through a telescope, an important factor in why its discovery took so long. This lack of visibility—hence lack of knowledge, for most people are not aware of Chiron's existence—is suggestive. Everyone has heard of the outer planets, but no one is able to see these planets without outside technical aid. Similarly, everyone feels the collective malaise, but they remain unaware of how to bridge the gap between the ego (the inner planets) and the collective (the outer planets), or how to make the collective less destructive by working with it in a philosophical and healing way. Some may dimly have heard that another planet has been discovered, but they usually have no idea of what its nature might be or where to find it in the solar system. Similarly, some people may have heard of such things as spiritual teachers, or of methods such as those found in Buddhism or Sufism, but they have no idea of how to bring such realities into their lives. They have not realized that in such legitimate teachings may lie the key to worlds beyond the ego, the bridge over the turbulent river of karma and misery, and even the key of how to work more appropriately with the world.

Put simply, Chiron's discovery indicates that we must admit to our need to be taught, that most of us cannot transcend ego alone. The need for a teacher has long been accepted in the East, so we can be encouraged that it is a tested principle. But it is difficult for the ego to accept such a teacher as

Chiron symbolizes because Chiron is somewhat wild, coming from outside the civilized realms of Saturn, and teaching,
it would seem, by this very outlandishness. Gurdjieff is an apt
example of such a teacher, and stories from both Sufi and Buddhist teachings also indicate that this "wildness" can become
an established tradition.

One of the interesting things about Chiron's orbit is its
irregularity. Due to its proximity to the much larger
astronomical bodies of Saturn and Uranus, it has marked per-
turbations in its orbit. No two of its orbits around the sun are
identical. This, and the fact that some astronomers think that
Chiron is not part of the original solar system,* indicate that
Chiron does not symbolize an energy that is part of the psychology of every human being. Unlike the other planets, it
is not part of our generic makeup.

This again relates it to the teaching function: someone from
outside serving as bridge from the realm of ego to that of non-
ego, or over the turbulent river of samsara, the life of suffering and blindness. Chiron is an energy that stimulates transformation as an outside agent. At the same time, though possibly
not of the original solar system, Chiron is presently *in* that
system, symbolizing that in some way the teaching function
is part of us. This paradox—that the catalyst is both part of
us and not part of us—is parallel to the notion that there is
both an inner guru and an external guru, or that the latter
stimulates in the student a recognition of his own basic enlightenment.

In terms of experience, then, Chiron symbolizes the function of an external teacher who, possibly through the various
facets of learning, leads the student onto a spiritual path which
will be a new direction in life, enabling him to work more
consciously and fully with the energies of Uranus, Neptune,
and Pluto. As in the myth, such a teacher can show us how

---

*Pluto, due to the radical declination of its orbit with respect to the plane
of the ecliptic in which the other planets move, is also thought by some to
be a visitor to this solar system.

to be a proper warrior, a role which seems to include healing as well as bravery. The recent discovery of this planetoid suggests that there is a great need for this function at the present time, that people need to become conscious of their need to be taught about the spiritual path. This may run counter to some people's sense of American individualism and self-sufficiency, but these notions are ego-bound. Chiron teaches us to be warriors, and the enemy seems to be ego. Chiron also teaches us to be healers, and this may turn out to be the same thing. Chiron teaches us the philosophical perspective, and the perspective that our wildness, which may put us outside the status quo, may be our wisdom.

The discovery of any planet affects the system of astrological sign rulerships. Whereas the discovery of Uranus introduced a period of clear imbalance both psychologically and socio-culturally, the discovery of any planets after that may be seen as leading toward a new order. Each new body introduces a new sign ruler, and thus leads toward each planet ruling only one sign.

In the case of Chiron, although not a full-bodied planet, one of the suggested rulerships is over the sign of Virgo (the others seem to be Sagittarius and Scorpio). The relation between Virgo and Chiron seems clear: both are associated with healing and learning, particularly in situations of inequality as in a student-teacher relationship or between a guru and disciple. The connection between Virgo and Chiron is further appropriate because Virgo is one of the two remaining signs which must share its ruler (Taurus being the other sign, for which Transpluto has been suggested as a ruler*). Some astrologers do not think that Mercury is an appropriate ruler for Virgo, as it does not seem to cover the earthy qualities of the sign.

As the Piscean Age closes, a new ruler for Virgo, Pisces' zodiacal opposite, seems appropriate. It may symbolize a new, more objective perspective on the amorphous energies of the final sign. At the same time, the issues of purity and cleanli-

---

*See the glossary for an explanation of Transpluto.

ness in relation to health and human survival are crucial to our time: the Age of Pisces seems to have been one in which material has been absorbed to a dangerous degree, which in some sense is understandable because of Pisces' absorbent nature. But as Pluto moves through the sign of Scorpio, this poisoning is coming to the surface. Our need for purification through a wider perspective is necessary, and this could be indicated by the rulership of Chiron.

Chiron is also related to the Virgo-Pisces axis through its connection to self-sacrifice. Mythically, Chiron gave up his immortality so that Prometheus might keep his. (He had good reason to do so, as he had been accidentally, though incurably wounded by one of Hercules' poison arrows.) Further, as the teacher of the Greek healer Asclepias ("unceasingly gentle"), he is related to the compassionate qualities of the final sign; from the standpoint of mythology, he certainly didn't lack the precision associated with Virgo. His name is apparently derived from the root "chir" meaning "hand" (thus connecting Chiron in a curious way with Mercury, the present ruler of Virgo). Finally, as an outsider Chiron is appropriate to a sign whose mythic background includes not only virgins but also harlots or any unowned woman.[12]

If we assign Chiron to the rulership of Virgo, we need only one more rulership—for Taurus—to bring us to a new stasis. Some have suggested Transpluto, which has been connected by some astrologers with wealth. The implications of a new ruler for Taurus would seem to be that, having been catalyzed into traveling the path beyond ego, we need to return to some practical grounding to learn more about the management of the material world. Possibly, too, Transpluto would indicate something "beyond death." After having traveled the path of complete transformation, the Buddha pointed to the earth as a witness to what he had discovered. The Buddha is traditionally associated with the sign of Taurus,* but this

---

*The Buddha is said to have been born at the time of a new moon in Taurus, in about 563 BCE. His birthday is today celebrated worldwide during late May or early June when the sun is astrologically in the sign of Gemini. At that time, astronomically, the sun is physically between the Earth and the constellation of Taurus.

gesture coming after his journey contains a hint of something grounded that can be found after commitment to the path that journeys beyond ego. The wealth beyond death is found, perhaps, in the depths of earth.

Thus this new ordering would be (eliminating the corulers and including only the new rulerships):

Aries	Mars	Libra	Venus
Taurus	Transpluto	Scorpio	Pluto
Gemini	Mercury	Sagittarius	Jupiter
Cancer	Moon	Capricorn	Saturn
Leo	Sun	Aquarius	Uranus
Virgo	Chiron	Pisces	Neptune

The Present Age: A Seed Period

The paradigm presented here for human consciousness and evolutionary development is based on the order of the planetary system with Pluto as the outermost planet. As such, it is subject to modification if new planets are discovered. At the present state of human development, however, the archetypal pattern of human consciousness seems to be as described.

Since 1978, Pluto is actually moving within the orbit of Neptune. While this does not alter the basic pattern described, it does have profound implications for current approaches to the development of consciousness. It suggests the need for a different emphasis in dealing with current problems, both on collective and individual level. With Pluto in Scorpio, these nuances are particularly pressing.

I have said before that the energies of Neptune must be properly cultivated if one is to make positive use of Pluto: compassion and egolessness must be felt in the heart, accepted and worked with; one must submit to something greater to make appropriate use of Plutonian power. Such power in the service of ego leads to mass (Neptune) devastation (Pluto). With Neptune now the outermost planet, the implication is that giving birth to compassion itself first requires some attention to the repolarizing process. One must die to oneself, be emotionally purged, if one is to manifest compassion. Perhaps this emphasis is now necessary because of the way in which individualism has been stressed in Western societies (this may well continue into the Aquarian Age when Leo will be the polar opposite sign).

A negative manifestation of this situation may be that electronic or technological knowledge (Uranus) gets into the hands of certain men of power (Pluto) whose aim is to create mass hopelessness and delusion (Neptune). The way to guard against this, as before, is accepting the energies on as conscious a level as possible, and making that our commitment.

Pluto's encroachment may make its issue more pressing (although this could also be a manifestation of Pluto in Scorpio). At the present time, Pluto as a collective factor appears on all sides: in the mid-1980s in the death of millions in Ethiopia; in various forms of abduction on the public mind (e.g., of children, in hijacking); the surfacing of the issue of child abuse; the enormity of the toxic waste problem; in renewed power plays over nuclear armaments; and in the plague mentality associated with the immune-system disease AIDS.

It seems we are called upon to be absolutely unflinching and honest in exploring the Plutonian underworld. Pluto presents that world before our eyes, as if to make the point clear. This, it seems, is our prime responsibility and must precede any effort to be compassionate. The reason is that without examining our personal underworld, we would simply poison our compassion, rendering it more harmful than if we did nothing. Pluto fuses polarities, and it seems that whenever we act on a polarized basis we can easily do more harm than good. As Jung pointed out, whenever we think we bring "good" into the world, we also bring a corresponding "evil."

Taking a more hopeful point of view, compassion and self-sacrifice (Neptune) can be empowered when they are based on a repolarization of the egocentric point of view. This is the positive side of the empowerment of delusion. Compassion can become far more than a mere gesture. It can take on the power to transform the face of the world (and, perhaps, the underworld, too).

Dane Rudhyar calls these "seed periods," times of "fecundation," and says that they have "marked crucial, long term events."[13] His interpretations are convincing but tend to emphasize the social or historical level. This is appropriate, because all of the previous periods occurred before Neptune and Pluto had been discovered, before the energies they symbolize became available for widespread, conscious development. The explanation given here is in psychological terms—or it attempts to relate the psychological to the sociological—and as such applies specifically to the present day when the need to take these matters personally is pressing.

According to Rudhyar, the current "fecundation" began in 1978, which curiously coincides with the 1977 discovery of Chiron. It is worth considering, therefore, that we may need teachers to help us interpret the needs of the present time, to help us bridge the gap between Saturn and Uranus, and then to understand the relationship between compassion and personal ego death, to enable us to give new life (Pluto) to the much-needed energy of egolessness and consequent compassion.

Put another way, the current period is one in which, in order to save the world at the end of the Age of Pisces, we must first bring all hidden things to the surface. We must die to old ways of doing things, thus giving birth to a level of consciousness that does not depend on ego-structure and ego security. The breakdowns we see on every side are the signs that all of this is necessary. These breakdowns are also the impetus, containing the energy which can bring about a collective rebirth.

6

The Roots and the Leaves, I: Emotion and Relationship

Our Common Situation

And O there are days in this life worth life and worth death. And O what a bright old song it is, that O 'tis love, 'tis love, 'tis love, that makes the world go round.
Charles Dickens

The old Lakota was wise. He knew that man's heart away from nature becomes hard; he knew that lack of respect for growing, living things soon led to lack of respect for humans, too.
Chief Luther Standing Bear
Lakota tribe

In the previous chapter the instability of the world as symbolized by the relationship of the planets to the signs was discussed. There were two interwoven emphases: the significance of this instability in individual spiritual development; and the significance for the world situation generally, or for the human condition as reflected in collective consciousness. It remains for us to examine a particular result of the general instability and explore the astrological implications of ways to work with it from a nonegoistic standpoint.

In contemporary Western society, one of the most common appearances of this instability is in the difficulty of maintaining fulfilling, long-term intimacies. There is a widespread questioning of the viability of the institution of marriage, and even the possibility of finding fulfillment in or through partnership is questioned. John Welwood, transpersonal psychologist, writes:

> The difficulty of finding and maintaining a healthy enduring relationship with a partner of the opposite sex has become a major life problem for increasing numbers of people today. Not only have the old ties holding couples together been rapidly dissolving, but the very notions of interdependence between men and women, and even heterosexuality itself have come under increasing scrutiny, if not downright attack. It is hard to even think clearly about the nature of the problem without falling prey to stereotypes, cliches, myths and fantasies of all kinds.[1]

We may say that this difficulty and instability mirror the more general problems of modern life, that the precariousness of the human situation is naturally being reflected in our personal lives. We may feel that it is quite natural for a person's life to reflect the conditions in which he or she lives and struggles. But if we are correct, have we really deepened our understanding of the problem?

We can only go so far by putting the blame on the "unnaturalness" of the present social, economic, and ecological situation. The pain of broken intimacy is not alleviated by referring it to a nonpersonal level. Abstract justifications generally do little to alleviate suffering; so although we can use statistics to demonstrate how our personal difficulties have sociological, political, or historical causes, this does not bring us to the psychological root of the matter.

Such approaches tend to be just more elaborate descriptions of the problem. Furthermore, when we consider the leviathan-like nature of the current economic and political situation, the way it seems to be both protean and all-pervasive, focusing on just how it all affects us can be more confusing than helpful. It's like blaming the rain for the floods: you may be right, but how much help is it in a storm?

The spectrum of viewpoints on the current instability in intimate partnerships has two endpoints. One is that the instability is harmful, perhaps decadent, probably immoral. Those who hold this opinion point to the effect of broken homes on young children and the effect of trauma on the parents themselves. The objections may also include religious views which say that the purpose of intimacy is to produce children, or that marriage is primarily a social function which it is one's duty to uphold.

From the other end of the spectrum this instability is seen as a positive sign, an indication that a new kind of intimacy is beginning to manifest or is required. The breakdown of old forms of intimacy will be seen as necessary in order to allow new forms to come forth. The new forms are seen as necessary because man's evolution would be restricted by old forms that have outlived their usefulness. New wine, says this point of view, cannot be put into old skins.

These could both be called "historical" perspectives insofar as the present situation is viewed in terms of the nonpresent—in terms of what has happened already or what has not happened yet. In the second viewpoint, the view of the future may often be given in astrological terms, using the symbolism of the coming Age of Aquarius. The first viewpoint is often stated in sociological terms, with a value put on the existing status quo. Both perspectives have value, and both contain obvious misconceptions, but somehow, neither gets to the heart of the matter. The historical approach may be interesting, intellectually stimulating, but it tends to be impersonal.

Whether the situation is viewed as a sign of regression and decadence or of hope and progress, it is clearly associated with suffering. Some may say that this suffering is necessary for our collective growth, others that it is a retribution for our wrongdoing. The truth may be some combination of the two, or it may be something else entirely. The main point seems to be that suffering rarely contributes significantly to growth unless the source of the suffering is examined. Historical analysis is useful insofar as it enables us to see the suffering with more perspective, but if we allow this to shield us from the visceral quality of our feelings, it becomes counterproductive. James Joyce, the Irish writer, once described history as a nightmare from which one is trying to awaken.[2] One nightmarish quality of history is that we are bound within its world, kept there by the wrathful demons of our thought patterns, the concepts which shield us from the true nature and cause of human suffering, yet which are so painful in themselves. History is created by ego.

In this chapter traditional astrological symbolism is used to shed light on current problems of intimacy. This symbolism is a language in itself; some translation is required. But in its fully stated form, the premise is that these problems result from a misunderstanding and misplacement of those energies symbolized by Cancer, the Moon, and the fourth house.

There is no one word that will cover all the ground of this complex of symbols. The word "emotion" seems closest, as long as it is understood in its most basic sense as "strong, generalized feeling" that "moves out" (from the Latin *emovere*).[3] That is, emotion is here seen as an energy that "moves out generally" or in no specified direction. This implies a center from which the moving out proceeds. As will become clear, this is quite appropriate. For the sake of clarity, this sense of the term will simply be called "emotion."

The astrological symbolism suggests that this energy was originally, and should be primarily, a nonpersonal, generalized feeling state imbuing man's intimacies with richness, but this energy has its origin and home elsewhere. Emotion could be said to be "in" our intimacies but not "of" them. Put simply, emotion was originally a relation to the earth itself, to the common source of all life, the common sense of center. The quote from Luther Standing Bear at the beginning of this section puts the matter quite succinctly.

People in our society, having lost a true relationship with the earth, seem to believe that emotion primarily belongs and originates in human relationship. We put a tremendous amount of energy, feeling, and anguish into our intimate partnerships, often seeing them as our ground or root in the world. There is too often a sense of desperation that bespeaks a pre-existing alienation. We try to solve this alienation through intimacy. But though these intimacies may serve as a temporary expedient, the astrological symbolism suggests that they do not get at the alienation itself. This may be because they rise out of a search that is based *in* that alienation in the first place.

From an astrological perspective, the situation isn't at all hopeless. The astrological symbols can give us a deeper understanding of the energies involved in the problem, thus giving a more encompassing perspective. To begin with, the symbolism shows that the feelings we bring to and encounter in relationship are only a small part of the "generalized feeling" of emotion itself, which is much vaster and more encompassing and needs to be recognized as such. One aspect of this is our relationship to the earth, but as we will see there are other levels of meaning of the lunar complex of symbols. These will allow us to reconnect to this emotional source even if the earth matrix level seems poisoned. Though Luther Standing Bear stood much closer to the cycles of the natural world than does the modern city dweller, the energy which he speaks of is accessible even to those who walk on concrete and cement all the time.

We will not, then, find our emotion simply through intimacy, but we *may* find fulfilling intimacy by finding the source and home of our emotions. We will need to accept, however, that emotion is a great power, much vaster than we have heretofore acknowledged. It is not primarily dualistic, though it may break down into dualistic feelings such as love-hate or attraction-repulsion. Coming into contact with its power within us may be somewhat humbling, but it may be just this power and humbling that is the real cure for the hubris-generated anguish which pervades our world on all levels, particularly and so poignantly in our intimacies.

Basic Symbols

Thus the superior man is careful
In the differentiation of things,
So that each finds its place.
                                        I Ching

Astrology differentiates the energy of intimate partnerships from the energy of emotion. Partnerships are symbolized in the horoscope in various ways: by the descendant, the seventh house, the planet Venus, and the sign Libra. Emotion is symbolized by the nadir, the fourth house, the Moon, and the sign Cancer.

The astrologer will recognize here the traditional system of planetary rulerships, in which Libra, ruled by the planet Venus, is associated with the seventh house and the descendant. Cancer, ruled by the Moon, is similarly associated with the fourth house and the nadir. These symbols are not interchangeable. The Moon, for example, is a distinct symbol from Cancer. Nevertheless, each group of related symbols is useful for a study which views astrology as an integrated system, not only as a means of interpretation. Our search is not for primarily interpretive explications, but for the life meanings that emerge from the symbols in themselves, and which must serve as a basis for any proper interpretation.

The relationship between these two groups of symbols is depicted in Botticelli's masterpiece "The Birth of Venus," which shows Venus rising from a seashell. The shell is traditionally associated with the sign of Cancer (the Crab protecting its inner sensitivities with a shell), which is associated with personal feeling states that are vulnerable and need protection from external harm or shock. Venus (Aphrodite) symbolizes love or non-coercive bonding;[4] she rises from the watery substrate of emotions—the universal ocean—via the subjective feelings; but she is clearly distinct from both universal emotion and personal feeling.

Because Venus rules Libra and the seventh house, we could say that Botticelli's painting depicts seventh-house astrological symbols "rising up" from the symbolism of the fourth house. The water below extends Cancerian symbolism into universality; and water is of course symbolically connected with emotion on various levels. Venus rises into the air, which is appropriate to its rulership of the air sign Libra.*

In the classical image, then, we see the distinct human energies of emotion and relationship (or "strong, generalized feeling" and "partnership") in symbolic form. We can expand the symbolism by referring to Hesoid's *Theogony*, where Aphrodite (the Greek figure corresponding to the Roman Venus) is born from the severed genitals of Uranus.[5] The blood from the wound became the Furies, reminiscent of the "open enemies" associated with the Venus-ruled seventh house. The Furies are also reminiscent of Mars, and thus of the Mars-ruled first house, the polar opposite and complement of the seventh. The myth symbolizes the polarity of the life of relationship.

Polarity comes into existence when emotions "surface," when they touch the external world. Strong, generalized feeling begins to pick and choose, to divide itself up; whereas in its basic nature emotion is not dualistic but unifying. The Moon symbolizes becoming part of or immersed in something more encompassing. Problems arise when the dualism of the feelings—love and hate, for example—is mistaken for the unifying power of emotion. Even our language fails to distinguish the two, as *Webster's Twentieth Century Dictionary* includes particularized, dualistic feelings in its definition of emotion. Astrological language is more precise in this area, with these two aspects of emotion being symbolized separately. So even our language serves as a barrier to inner understanding.

The surfacing of emotion into the dualistic world of self-

---

*See the glossary under Elements for an explanation of signs associated with elements.

and-other is symbolized by the horizon of the birthchart, sometimes called the *event horizon*.

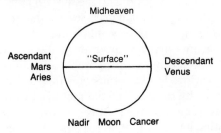

The first and seventh houses, ruled respectively by Mars and Venus, both begin at the horizon, at points equidistant from the nadir,* the point which symbolizes the deepest sustainment of the individual. If we move counterclockwise from the ascendant, we find that the cardinal points of ascendant, nadir, and descendant correspond to the progress of the myth. The genitals (Mars/ascendant) fall into the ocean (nadir) and rise up into the air as Venus (Libra/descendant). Between the ascendant and descendant is the emotional source which connects the "I" persona of the ascendant to the "other" of the descendant through the deeper sense of identity, sustainment, and connection, symbolized at the nadir. That is, the relationship takes place along the horizon, but emotion itself lies at the nadir. Or, we might say that relationships take place along the horizon, but the deeper sense of relatedness is found at the nadir.

Venus is primarily a symbol of interpersonal affairs. She functions through polarity: there must be an "I" and an "other" or, as seen through her rulership of Libra, a sense of value which can be weighed. Her polarized nature becomes clear if she is subjected to stress. Her love needs or demands return, and if there is no return love becomes empty polarity, opposition, and strife. Mythically, Venus was allied with Mars during the Trojan War, and their intercessions were by no means always peaceful.

A certain amount of stress seems necessary for growth. This

---

*See the glossary for an explanation of equidistance.

is particularly evident in the physical stress of athletic training. If a muscle is subjected to too much stress, its optimum performance abruptly turns into exhaustion: strength becomes its opposite. According to astrology, stress or challenge is needed in intimate partnerships as well; this is what lies behind the accepted notion that the most enduring love partnerships are those which combine compatible or harmonious energies with less harmonious, possibly stress-producing energies. A certain amount of challenge or stress is deemed healthy for the partnership; but if there is too much, exhaustion sets in. Similarly, when seventh-house energies are overstressed or overloaded, they turn into their opposites, the dark side, the Furies.

A circuit that is carrying more than it is meant to either blows a fuse or throws a circuit-breaker. When this happens, people are literally and symbolically left in the dark. Similarly, if Venus is overly stressed or "overloaded," the normal circuit of emotion and relation is broken; people "are cast out into outer darkness" with "weeping and gnashing of teeth,"[6] which means disorder, suffering, and severed connections. The circuit of emotion and relation begins at the nadir, the source and home of emotion. The energy then rises into and permeates relationship and partnership symbolized at the descendant, and these become the basis for social structures and a person's full work in the world.

The mistake we often make is to assume that our emotion has its source in our intimate partnerships, or that it can find sustainment there. If we try to pour all our emotional energy through those partnerships, we will experience overload, blown fuses, broken circuits. If partnerships are the only place where our emotion finds outlet, it may be a sign that it has not found its proper place, its home. Metaphorically, if our emotion spends all its time in our intimacies, it may be a sign that our emotion is spending too much time away from home.

People leave when life at home is no longer viable. Perhaps the home is ruined, poisoned, divided, or torn apart. We would do well, therefore, to look to the condition of our home. The astrological point referring to both home and emotion is the nadir, and by extension the fourth house.

Emotion, Earth and the Fourth House

Fourth house experiences tell basically what the human being is as a concrete, actual person. These personal foundations condition what the individual will be able to express, love or hate, procreate or create.
                                        Dane Rudhyar

The aspects of life associated with the nadir and the fourth house may seem varied and disconnected at first glance. They include home, family, relation to one's past, to tradition, and to one's most intimate personal life. Also symbolized by these are real estate, considered in a nonspeculative or nontransferable sense, and one's early experience of nurture and childhood. In addition, this sector of the horoscope is associated with the end of life and with one's "deepest sustainment and most secure foundation."[7] The connection with nurturance and with real estate leads to the common association of the fourth house with Mother Earth.

These seemingly disparate areas of life are not a group of different energies as they might seem, but varying manifestations of a single energy. We might say that one's personal emotions and feeling for the earth (nontransferable real estate and most secure foundation) have the same source. Tradition also supplies a sense of deep personal sustainment. The different levels of a house's manifestation may be likened to the many facets of one jewel: we might say that by entering the house from one door, the jewel reflects light in a certain way whereas if one enters from another door, it might at first appear to be a different jewel. Closer inspection reveals otherwise.

Metaphorically, we might say that the astrological houses are centrally heated. If one room is cold, the rest of the house will be cold as well. All the heat comes from one source. In other words, if we find that any one of the energies in a house is stifled, it is worth checking to see if the other energies are stifled as well. If we find, in this case, that the earth is barren and increasingly torn up, we can expect this (a fourth-house matter) to be reflected in the deepest strata of our being, in our sense of deepest personal sustainment, and in our emotion. According to the astrological symbolism, it is quite understandable that techno-industrial civilization goes hand in hand with a destruction of the earth, even as the people suffer internally from a breakdown of the family unit, a loss of connection to "home ground," and widespread emotional dislocation.

Chapter Seven presents some brief examples from history of how emotion has been connected to the land, to the cyclic, nontransferable earth. Industrial-technological civilization is causally connected to a pervasive sense of emotional dislocation and disconnection; for though the poets of this linear technological civilization may celebrate the sustainments of nature, they do so from outside the mainstream which is flowing rapidly toward the falls where emotion is harnessed for power.

When emotion, which is primarily an inner energy, emerges and metaphorically walks on the surface of the earth (as opposed to residing within), it will of its nature wish to retain a connection with its cyclic, living source. But if the surface of the earth is no longer life-giving or life-supporting, to what container will emotion flow?

Emotion is, of course, highly sensitized. This is the significance of Cancer's shell: a protection against harsh externals. The outer world is increasingly sharp-edged these days, full of Uranian tools and Saturnian structures with square edges. How will emotion—or emotional people, which means all of us—respond to such a world?

There would seem to be three characteristic responses. The first, found in very few, is to love and embrace the world completely as it is, with all its sharp edges and its poisons, without fear of being cut, wounded, or made sick. Perhaps the earth is no longer a container for the emotions, but people who respond in this open way may point out that loving the earth is like pouring water into a sieve over a pond. The sieve may be a poor container, but nothing is really lost because the pond connects the water to a still larger container, the ocean itself. To many, this larger container may not be visible, but we may take this sort of response as an ideal, the Buddhist attitude of a bodhisattva.

Most of us find it difficult to be so open: the spirit may be willing, but there is resistance. We have a natural tendency to protect ourselves, to hold ourselves back from complete openness. Yet willingness to be wounded by the world and courage to accept openness is integral to our ability to have fulfilling relationships. Openness is the basis of our relationship to our own emotional state as well, accepting the violent and the peaceful, the loving and the angry, thus opening the door to some sort of clear seeing not muddied by preconceptions or judgments. How will we relate truly if we do not see clearly, or commit ourselves to move toward clear seeing?

The second characteristic response to the barren sharpness of the world is to stifle all emotional response. If emotion is like the waters of a river, this response might be likened to forcing the river to flow backwards, or at least damming it up. As with water in dams and hydroelectric plants, stifling emotion seems very useful, and those who do so may make the most reliable of workers—unless the dam breaks.

When waters are dammed up, vast reservoirs collect behind the dams. People may still build homes beneath such structures and stake their lives on the structure's holding together. But because any apparent stability lies beneath tons of contained water, the water itself appears threatening. So it is with dammed-up emotion. If its natural flow has been checked too severely, it has the power to carry away all the defensive structures in the life of a person who chooses to live beneath the dam. Seen this way, emotion itself is not to be feared but rather its artificial stifling.

Such a situation is threatening, and people living that way will tend to keep their protective structures in good repair. It is considered immensely good fortune if the dam never breaks. Then one never has to "deal with the emotions" any more than one has to deal with the dark and the cold; for the dam not only protects one from emotion (metaphorically), but also supplies light and heat. Thus one is cut off from natural life and ego depends on this artificial structure and its limitations.

The third characteristic response to the perceived barrenness of the world is to shift the current of emotion from one channel into another. Confronted with an earth of so many nonliving things, we shift the energy onto the nearest living receptor, usually the human being with whom we are most intimately united. Intimate partnership then becomes a channel for the vast flow of emotional energy that once related directly to the cycles of nature. At one time, the "nearest living receptor" would have been the vast panorama of living nature, the living earth moving in its slow, intelligent cycles. Now that these cycles have been broken down into man-made, linear, goal-directed projects, human life has lost its organic sustainment. The nearest living receptor is now likely to be another human being and partnership becomes the narrow channel for the seaward flow of emotion.

It is interesting that except for human beings, our world appears to have room for fewer and fewer creatures. It has even been suggested that evolution is now focused on the developing consciousness of man. Humans may have proliferated at the expense of other life forms. It does not seem at all strange, then, that we shift onto our fellows the energy-current that was once directed to life forms and cycles that are no longer viable.

Problems arise because emotion is much more powerful than we are usually willing to admit or recognize. It does not pass easily through the narrow channels of another human heart. The attempt to force it through often results in the appropriately named "broken heart." Human beings are sensitive transformers: the broad Amazon does not fit through the heart's ventricles. Though the very attempt to redirect the energy flow shows that the current is still seeking the ocean, the result of the flood is often destruction and the breakdown of security, which leads to the enforced confrontation with the power of our emotion and of the emotional qualities that relate us to the world.

Seen another way, the shift of emotional current is like taking a pain killer to alleviate the suffering we feel when emotion touches the harsh edges of the world. Modern pain killers do not provide permanent solutions because they do not set right the imbalance which is at the root of the pain. Similarly, the search for emotional fulfillment through the single channel of our intimacies is futile. This course is essentially a buffer to shield us from our isolation, and like a sick person taking aspirin, we may feel better, go outside, play in the world, only to find out later that something fundamental has been disregarded, possibly leaving one even worse off than before.

So we must look to a deeper connection. Intimacy must partake of a deeper relatedness that is available to us, not simply cover up our basic loneliness.

Those who have shifted emotional energy onto their intimate partnerships may not be aware that they have done so. This is because the shift is completely condoned in our culture. It is encouraged, taught in the schools, lauded in romantic novels and in the media, and applauded by parents. The habit is quite ingrained, and we seek no alternatives.

Because of this, many will maintain that any attempt to divorce intimacy and emotion must indicate lack of feeling. The point to be made, however, is not that intimacy and emotion are like two ships which must pass in the night and never meet, but rather that emotion gives birth to intimacy, instead of the other way around, and that intimacy cannot contain all our emotion. This statement is not meant to denigrate intimacy, but simply to clarify a natural situation (as indicated by astrological and mythological symbolism)—that emotion has tremendous power. Differentiating emotion from intimacy is not meant to be unfeeling, but simply to enable us to see our lives more clearly, to separate in order to understand, to understand in order to live more fully and effectively. Such clarity allows us to be fulfilled, to find fulfillment in self-understanding.

The intention is summed up quite well in *I Ching* hexagram number sixty-four: *Wei Chi* (Before Completion). Its symbol is fire over water, which seems an apt designation for a time like the present which can be symbolized by the Cuyahoga River in Ohio catching fire in the 1970s from the chemical spills that polluted it. The hexagram speaks directly to my point. The section entitled "The Image" reads:

> Fire over water:
> The image of the condition before transition.
> Thus the superior man is careful
> In the differentiation of things,
> So that each finds its place.[8]

These words help us understand the "differentiation of things". Also, the precession of astrological ages places us at an important "condition before transition," as we move out of the Piscean Age into the Age of Aquarius. The hexagram is quite hopeful, despite an apparent state of confusion. In his analysis of this hexagram, translator Richard Wilhelm writes:

> . . . order stands pre-formed within, despite
> the outward appearance of complete disorder.[9]

The current disorder in human intimacy may be a situtation "before completion," containing within its disorder all the elements necessary for a new ordering and ongoing growth— for successful transition. We are warned, however, against overly facile solutions: The "Judgment" reads:

> Before completion. Success.
> But if the little fox, after nearly
> completing the crossing,
> Gets his tail in the water,
> There is nothing that would further.[10]

So we must not rely too much on assurance. We cannot simply say, "It's all right if intimacy breaks down. The Age of Aquarius is about to dawn." This would obviously be pure escapism. On the other hand, we need not condemn ourselves or the times for the confusion we see, for in the current conditions and in ourselves—in fact, as part of our confusion itself —is the potential to create new order, new growth. Wilhelm's interpretation is worth quoting:

> The conditions are difficult. The task is great and full of responsibility. It is nothing less than that of leading the world out of confusion, back to order. But it is a task that promises success because there is a goal that can unite the forces now tending in different directions. . . Therefore one must separate things in order to unite them.[11]

The "goal that can unite the forces now tending in different directions" may be a deeper understanding of the basis of our intimacies, a process which may be inseparable from finding a new connection to the earth itself, or to the nurturing energies which it both symbolizes and embodies. The purpose of this study is to show how this might be done, which requires an examination of the initial process of alienation.

To accomplish this, it is necessary to "separate things in order to unite them." A doctor needs to understand the illness before he can cure it, and we are all our own physician. The healing process here is to unite the polarity again, to reconcile the endpoints and so achieve completion, which, in the *I Ching* as elsewhere, involves movement. The first step in this process is to examine some of the less common associations of the nadir and the fourth house. Through these we may come to a deeper understanding of the unifying power of emotion.

The Center

> *Things fall apart; the centre cannot hold;*
> *Mere anarchy is loosed upon the world, . . .*
> William Butler Yeats

As many astrological writers have pointed out, the symbolism of the fourth house and nadir focuses on the idea of a center. Physically, this center is our globe, the center of which is geographically the same for all people. Dane Rudhyar writes:

> In the fourth house the person can and should reach the experience of center—the center of his own global, total personality as well as the center of global humanity, of a firmly established and concretely real brotherhood of man.[12]

We can also speak of a psychological center, an area of consciousness which will be the same for all. This is the collective unconscious, also associated with the fourth house. Robert Hand, astrologer, writes:

Most important, the fourth house represents what is buried in the psychological sense: the unconscious mind. We are referring not to Freud's notion of a personal unconscious as much as to Jung's notion of a collective unconscious. The collective unconscious is common to all humanity simply by the fact of our all being biologically similar. It is not a function of individual experience but comes through either heredity or experiences that are absolutely inevitably common to us all regardless of cultural or individual variations.[13]

And further:

At the innermost level, the fourth house symbolizes the psychic functions that connect us to the rest of life. It governs feelings of belonging, being at home in, and being connected. It is our link to the collective unconscious, to the psychological patterns that we share with all human beings.[14]

Just as the earth nurtures all beings with physical substance, so the collective unconscious nurtures all beings in their psychological wholeness. The distinction between physical substance and the workings of the psyche is used here for the purpose of discussion, though the two are basically inseparable, just as the various symbolic levels of an astrological house are essentially one meaning seen from various angles. Thus, if the earth is not nurturing us psychologically, we can expect that it is not nurturing us physically either, and vice versa. The contemporary situation shows this to be the case.

If we extend the symbolism of the fourth house, we come upon some interesting parallels with other traditions. Through these, we will be able to see the unifying power of the energy symbolized at the nadir (i.e., the emotions, the ecological well-being of the planet). Dane Rudhyar associates the nadir with the Midnight Sun and the center of the earth. Both of these bring to mind the image of a deeply centered fire, the molten center of the earth, the Sun located deep within a person's consciousness.

For example, there seems to be a parallel between the notion of an inner Sun and what we have been told of the Tibetan Buddhist practice of *tumo*, the Yoga of Inner Fire practiced by advanced adepts. Both speak to the immense power of emotion, the very power that makes human intimacy inadequate to contain the vast flow of emotional energy. The primary purpose of emotion is not simply directed into intimacy, but instead deals with unification. Lama Anagarika Govinda, authority on Tibetan Buddhism, writes:

> The fire of spiritual integration which fuses all polarities, all mutually exclusive elements arising from separateness of individuation, this is what the Tibetan word gTum-mo [tumo] means in the deepest sense, and what makes it one of the most important subjects of meditation. . . . It is the warmth of spiritual emotion which, if intensified, kindles the flame of inspiration, from which is born the power of renunciation and what appears to the outsider as asceticism. [15]

The progress from emotion through inspiration to asceticism parallels the astrological progression from emotion (fourth house) through personal creativity (fifth house) through the perfecting qualities of such things as health, purification, and grounded learning (sixth house). Lama Govinda continues:

> It is that emotion which in its lowest form is like a straw-fire, nourished by a momentary enthusiasm and blind urges, while in its highest form it is the flame of inspiration, nourished by spiritual insight, by true vision, by direct knowledge and inner certainty.
>
> Both have the nature of fire; but as little as the shortlivedness and the inferior force of a straw-fire negates the fact that the same element if directed into proper channels and supplied with an adequate fuel, is capable of melting the hardest steel—so we should not underestimate the force of emotion, because it may sometimes spend itself in short-lived enthusiasm. We should recognize that the warmth of emotion is inseparable from inspiration, a state in which we truly and completely forget ourselves in the experience of higher reality, an act of self-surrender which frees and transforms our innermost being. [16]

These words recall those of P.D. Ouspensky, a student of Gurdjieff:

> But one cannot be aware of oneself for fifteen minutes without a very strong emotional element. You must pro-

duce something that makes you emotional; you cannot do it without the help of the emotional centre.[17]

Ouspensky's use of the term "centre" here is not the same as the center of the earth referred to above. Nevertheless, we see in his words, and in those of Lama Govinda, that emotion is not something that comes into being as a result of human interaction or intimacy. It lies deeper, and for this reason it is central to any program of self-understanding. It is our most natural, deep-felt response to the world, that response which rises from within us before thought has time to enter with its attempts to rearrange things.

Because it is unpremeditated, emotion represents something true, natural, and real about our participation in the world. Also, because of this naturalness, we can learn a great deal from the challenge of emotion. Whether we like the experience or not, whether it is difficult or not, whether emotion makes us feel exalted, childish, overwhelmed, or merely impotent, it tells us a great deal about ourselves. If we observe emotional energy closely, we learn. Such observation or "self-remembering," as Ouspensky repeats again and again, is essential on any spiritual path: "...self-remembering is a necessary state in man's development....One has to pass through it."[18]

To be in touch with emotion is to realize that our entire world affects us at that level. Our intimate partnerships are part of that entire world, but they do not encompass all of it. Nevertheless, if we observe ourselves closely, we will see that our relationship to the entire world *is* basically emotional—a nonspecific moving outward—and we will see that emotion has its source at the very base of that relationship, providing a warmth of relatedness that can fill our entire life.

The problem in the modern age is that the world—at least the surface of the planet—doesn't seem emotionally receptive or able to be part of any emotional relatedness. It seems to be *we* who feel emotional, while the world (especially in cities) seems cut off, deprived of the natural cycles of life; then, because we too feel alienated, we project that feeling onto the earth. The cycle of emotional relatedness is disrupted, and people begin to regard the earth in a utilitarian way.

This naturally becomes stultifying, and we look for another

outlet that will receive our emotion. We spend so much time seeking this that we forget to "self-remember"; and when we *do* look for this self, our real nature, what do we find?

Fourth-house symbolism is helpful here, because it indicates who one is at the innermost level, beneath any level of social interaction. Rudhyar calls it the experience of "concrete self-hood," and if we follow the symbolism presented so far, this inner level, the root of the self, is not a narrow ego but the vastness of the collective unconscious, or the field of life as a whole, the sense of planetary family. Any notion of selfhood experienced at the fourth-house level must grow from and retain a close connection to that area of the psyche where all selves experience the world in the same symbolic terms. The self is here intimately connected to all other selves, and to the life of the planet itself. Ego loses its self-importance as it is faced with the collective memory of the race.

This ground is a bit tricky. We must beware of referring to the unconscious in a way that implies it to be conscious. Jung distinguishes between the archetypes of the collective unconscious and the archetypal images that appear in dreams or in daily experience. However, we can say at least that in the collective unconscious there is, in Lama Govinda's words, an "integration which fuses all polarities, all mutually exclusive elements arising from separateness of individuation." Here we can see the parallel between the Inner Fire, the Midnight Sun, and the collective unconscious; for in each symbol or process we find a fusion of polarity. In each, the individuated self is simultaneously lost and found; a new Self rises from its own ashes, which are the small self of ego.

Also, as we will see later in a different context, the whole notion of Mother Earth among certain tribal groups was an essential component of the process of individuation as they experienced it. People's identities both personally and as a group, were intimately bound by their connection to the land itself, a connection which made people what they were, as much as our own lack of connection makes us what we are.

This, then, is the center. But it is a strange sort of center, as we usually conceive centers. Our normal conception of center is of a point formed by the convergence of radii, a middle area surrounded (on all sides equally) by a larger area. However, when we say that the collective unconscious is the center, we see that this center is larger than the circumference. If the circumference is the world of the conscious mind, and the center is the collective unconscious, then those who live in harmony with the center do so in a larger world of consciousness than do those who live on the circumference.

The difficulty is resolved when we cease to think in dichotomies. The collective unconscious is coextensive with the world of surface consciousness; its contents appear in the conscious world as events. It is a mistake to think of the unconscious as a small, compacted central realm. The idea of the unconscious is not limited to what we know of the brain, for the mind is not the brain and not limited by it. The unconscious is the center of that circle whose center is everywhere and whose circumference is nowhere. This "center" functions through the fusing of polarities, a symbol of psychic integration mentioned in traditions as diverse as alchemy, tantricism, and gnosticism. This process of fusion seems necessary to anyone seeking in-depth integration, and therefore integration between one's self and the world.

The process is symbolized at the astrological nadir of the horoscope, the deepest point of the personal world, the emotional center of experience, the earth itself. The emotions are at the center because it is through emotional energy that such unity is found. By its very power, emotion enables us to see the unity of ourselves and our world. If one abandons oneself to that emotional power, it is possible to learn about the deepest "Self," beneath the level of conscious control. Thus, emotion has spiritual strength, and this strength is rooted in and symbolized by the living soil of earth, which Gautama Buddha called as witness to his enlightenment. Contacting and accepting this level of energy is essential to our ability to develop fulfilling, intimate relationships.

Ascendant-Descendant and Partnership

Hold fast enough to Quietness
And of the ten thousand things none but can be
worked on by you.

I have beheld them, whither they go back.
See, all things howsoever they flourish
Return to the root from which they grew.

                Tao Te Ching, *Chapter XVI*

Diagrams can help explain the relationship between emotion and intimacy. Partnerships are polarities, separate entities interacting. Intimacy indicates that two become one, that two are "connected." This can be depicted as a straight line with two end-points:

This is also a diagram of the ascendant-descendant axis. The end-points designate the intersection of the plane of experience with the cosmos. As a simple line segment, it symbolizes partnership without context. If the line is visualized as the cross-section of a plane—the plane of experience—it becomes more evident that this experience has no depth (ergo, no context). To give it depth, we add the rest of the circle (or sphere, if we retain the three-dimensional view).

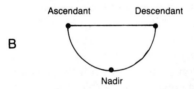

The ascendant indicates temperament (among other qualities): the most natural way for an individual to merge with his or her environment. The descendant indicates the resultant needs or tendencies in one-on-one partnership or intimacy. This is one's "other half" projected onto others, as well as the others themselves insofar as the individual is aware of them. One's personal development needs to go through a number of phases between temperament and intimacy, and these are symbolized by the first six houses in the horoscope (contained in the lower hemisphere).

In this chapter, the primary movement has been from the

first house (at the ascendant) through the nadir (fourth-house cusp) to the descendant (seventh-house cusp). Moving from first to second to third, and so forth, provides a picture of the unfolding of temperament through the realms and outreaches of experience. Using keywords, temperament (first house) generates a sense of personal value and values (second house), personal resources which generate a sense of immediate environment, and something about which to communicate (third house). This in turn becomes concretized into a personal feeling of home and belonging (fourth house). With this feeling one reaches out creatively (fifth house), and then, observing that personal creations are not complete in themselves, undergoes a process of self-criticism and adjustment (sixth house) in order to relate most fully with others (seventh house). This picture is obviously oversimplified. Various astrological texts give a more extensive treatment.[19] The main point is to reiterate the logic within the astrological symbols.

The progress through the first six houses also depicts the relationship between ascendant and descendant, self and other. There is this difference, however: here the descendant is not generated by a straight line (as in diagram A), but by an entire hemisphere or semicircle, which aptly symbolizes containment, the material from which growth may take place.

C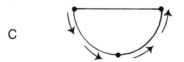

Pictorially, this is a bowl. By moving in a counterclockwise direction, a person's natural outreach comes to the stage of development which can be called intimacy and partnership after he or she has developed the inner integrity and rootedness necessary to contain energy. The crucial point in this development is the nadir, symbolically midway between the ascendant and descendant, moving along the circumference.

The house which this point initiates is ruled by the Moon, most particularly the astrological symbol for containment.*

Psychologically, then, a person cannot extend into true intimacy until he or she has found a point of essential sustainment or can contain energy. The depth of emotional centeredness must be found. Without this, relationship and intimacy exist only on the surface, and like the seed that falls on barren soil, they may spring up but will soon wither. Unless a person develops relationships or intimacies in the manner indicated in diagram C, the intimacies and relationships will be short-lived.

A possible objection to this schemata might be: Yes, but doesn't the Sun move from the ascendant in a clockwise direction? It rises into the twelfth house and progresses toward the midheaven at noon. Why not proceed in that direction instead?

This clockwise direction is a daily direction. It involves man's ephemeral deeds. It is also a direction with much spiritual potential, as suggested in a previous section ("Reversing the Wheel"). But the movement of the Sun into the twelfth house and then upward toward the midheaven is really somewhat illusory, because the Sun doesn't really "move through the houses." Rather, the houses move over the Sun. This movement comes from the Earth's turning. The Sun's own movement is counterclockwise, increasing in zodiacal longitude by approximately a degree a day. This movement of one degree per day becomes a movement of one degree per year in the progressed chart, which symbolizes the development of a man's seed-potential and inner growth. The implication is that

---

*Technically, the Moon is the ruler of the sign of Cancer which can be found on the cusp of any house of the horoscope, depending on the time of day the chart is cast. The fourth house is symbolically indicative of Cancerian matters, and in general is associated with the Moon, but any sign of the zodiac can be found on the fourth-house cusp. This discussion is concerned only with the symbolical dimension of the nadir as the seat of security (Moon) and the inner being (Cancer). It does not attempt to deal with the realities of any given horoscope.

our development of intimacy results from this inner developmental level, this growth of human potential, irrespective of external events. The intimacy thus becomes a soul mating, not a result of the chronological time measured by the Sun's apparent movement through the houses.

There is also an old notion that man's true development moves opposite to chronological time. Chronological time measures entropy: the breakdown and increasing disorder of biological features and fixtures, increased randomness, increased disorganization. Yet, as time passes, a human being may become increasingly aware of growth and development. This may be why the Buddha said (in the *Sutra of Forty-Two Chapters*) that the length of a man's life is not measured in days or by "the time that passes during a meal", but "by the breath".[20] And the breath is the ongoing link between the conscious and the unconscious, or, in terms of the symbolism used herein, between the horizon and the nadir. Of the breath, Lama Govinda wrote:

> The most important result of the practice of *anapanasati*, or 'mindfulness with regard to breathing,' is the realization that the process of breathing is the connecting link between conscious and subconscious, gross-material and fine-material, volitional and non-volitional functions, and therefore the most perfect expression of the nature of all life.[21]

Thus, growth in mind and spirit proceeds in the opposite direction from that of the body's dissolution.

If we proceed in a clockwise direction from the ascendant, we generate first the midheaven, and through it the descendant. This pattern of growth may be visualized in the following diagram:

D

Here one comes to intimate partnership only through public recognition. This is putting the cart before the horse, yet it

seems quite typical of our society, where people become intimate (or form intimate partnerships) through and as a result
of the work they do. Therefore we have many such partnerships which are based on "what I do" rather than on deep
"soul yearnings" or spiritual needs; partnerships of this type
are based on the establishment of ego via external structure
rather than a unifying sense of global family.

The idea seems prevalent today that a person should work
in the world at the expense of his or her personal development. People find their mates through their positions: the
somewhat uninspiring archetype of this myth is the captain
of the football team going out with the captain of the cheer-
leaders or movie stars marrying movie stars. This practice of
forming intimate partnerships with those we meet in the world
of affairs would be fine if all of our work included the energies
of our deepest integration. But as we know too well, much
of our work is soul-stultifying rather than fulfilling, and as
a result these "relationships based on world affairs" become
"affairs" in the sense of designatedly short-term encounters.
Either they don't last, or they last at the expense of personal
development.

A society based on such relationships would seem destined
to become soulless itself, symbolically, psychologically, and
ecologically. Also, the relationships themselves tend to be
empty and to end because people feel, despite their marriages
and their careers, that their lives are empty. This is symbolized in diagram D, seen now as a bowl turned upside down,
unable to contain anything. The diagram shows in simple
form the unhappy reality of "empty" marriages based on duty
and ambition (Saturnian qualities associated with the
midheaven). The epitome of such a situation is a husband's
career becoming the "soul" or deepest sustainment of a
marriage.

The midheaven and nadir of a horoscope, however, are not
separate entities but a partnership in themselves, symbolizing one of the basic polarities of human life. Each is necessary to the other, like darkness and light. In terms of daily,
worldly time, relationship will be generated via the midheav-
en: in the daily round, career supports the home. But in terms

of personal sustainment and full individual growth, relationship will be generated via the nadir. The symbol for this is the tree, which may have its fruit in heaven, but which has its roots in the underworld. Both worldly activity and personal sustainment should be integral and inseparable parts of our lives.

Imbalance can occur, however, if the inner world symbolized at the nadir is not given the same conscious attention and acceptance as the outer world symbolized at the midheaven. Most trees do not live if water only touches the leaves and fruit; it must reach the roots if the leaves are to remain healthy.

Simply put, we are overly concerned with action at the expense of feeling. The ideal of inaction is stated in the *Tao Te Ching:*

> The Valley Spirit never dies.
> It is named the Mysterious Female.
> And the Doorway of the Mysterious Female
> Is the base from which Heaven and Earth sprang.
> It is there within us all the while.
> Draw upon it as you will, it never runs dry.[22]

7

The Roots and the Leaves, II: Technology and the Living Earth

. . . for the nation's hoop is broken and scattered. There is no center any longer, and the sacred tree is dead.
Black Elk

If it is true that our emotional energy finds its most natural center in the matrix of the earth, and that the emotional dislocations of modern life indicate a lack of vital connection with that matrix, then a brief look at history should reveal examples of differences in emotional quality or stability between people rooted in earth and those uprooted from it. Such a comparison is not meant judgmentally. Imbalance may be indicative of and necessary to growth beyond ego. Still, there is an important distinction between creative and destructive imbalance, as between the neurotic and the person on the spiritual path (or, we might say, between using neurosis as energy on the path, or being used by it merely as neurosis). Spiritual growth demands some sort of stability, even if only as a basis for deeper exploration: the instability of such growth needs a firm foundation.

A lengthy examination of history is beyond the scope of this book. Two examples will serve to demonstrate the historical background of the situation being discussed. The common denominators of these examples are that both are related to the development of industry, the growth and spread of technology, the breakdown of the family unit, and of the relationship to the natural fecundity of earth. Both therefore show a deep sense of loss and disconnectedness. Finally, both reached their crucial development in the nineteenth century, and therefore may be seen astrologically as manifestations of the change in human awareness symbolized by the discovery of Uranus and Neptune.

In 1829, Thomas Carlyle, English essayist and historian, referred to his age as "above all others, the Mechanical Age...which with its whole, undivided might, forwards, teaches, and practices the great art of adapting means to ends."[1] That is, the period was functional, and as such has strong parallels with Dane Rudhyar's description of the cooperation symbolized by the seventh house:

> The cooperators should feel that their "operation in common serves a purpose within a larger unit of existence, normally within a particular social community, or at most within mankind considered as a social organism. It should be a *functional* participation. One should find implied in the relationship between two partners an at least dim realization of what the relationship is *for*, what is its purpose...[2]

Carlyle's description also points to the way men were disconnected from the natural processes symbolized by the nadir:

> We war with rude Nature; and, by our resistless engines, come off always victorious, and loaded with spoils.[3]

He goes on to speak of the pervasive effect of such a situation:

> These things, which we state lightly enough here, are yet of deep import, and indicate a mighty change in our whole manner of existence. For that same habit regulates not our modes of action alone, but our modes of thought and feeling.[4]

Nineteenth-century poetry clearly reflects this change. In 1798, Wordsworth wrote in "Lines Composed a Few Miles Above Tintern Abbey":

> Knowing that Nature never did betray
> The heart that loved her; 'tis the privilege
> Through all the years of this our life, to lead
> From joy to joy; for she can so inform
> The mind that is within us, so impress
> With quietness and beauty, and so feed
> With lofty thoughts, that neither evil tongues,
> Rash judgments, nor the sneers of selfish men,
> Nor greetings where no kindness is, nor all
> The dreary intercourse of daily life,
> Shall e'er prevail against us . . . .[5]

Matthew Arnold, who was a great admirer of Wordsworth, wrote in a very different tone. Some sixty-nine years later he spoke of a very different relationship with nature:

> The Sea of Faith
> Was once, too, at the full, and round earth's shore
> Lay like the folds of a bright girdle furled.
> But now I only hear
> Its melancholy, long, withdrawing roar,
> Retreating, to the breath
> Of the night wind, down the vast edges drear
> And naked shingles of the world.
>
> Ah, love, let us be true
> To one another! for the world, which seems
> To lie before us like a land of dreams,
> So various, so beautiful, so new,
> Hath really neither joy, nor love, nor light,
> Nor certitude, nor peace, nor help for pain;
> And we are here as on a darkling plain
> Swept with confused alarms of struggle and flight
> Where ignorant armies clash by night.[6]

Arnold's voice is alienated from fourth-house energies; even the sea, the great symbol of the source of life and unity, is for him a symbol of separation. And, most significantly, his sense of disconnection induces him to reaffirm the bond of intimacy, seeking there either solace or reconnection. "Dover Beach" stands, then, as a fine example of the shift of emotional current away from the symbolism of the nadir toward the intimacies symbolized at the seventh house. Arnold's faith is no longer in nature, but in human connections.

In America, the nineteenth century was also a time when people were torn from the rootedness of earth. The conquest of the American continent was completed during this period, and it might be described as a no longer rooted people (immigrant Europeans) conquering the more rooted cultures of the Native Americans. There are a number of facets of this conquest that relate directly to the present study.

First and foremost is the attitude of Native American peoples to the earth. The *Curriculum Materials Resource Unit* of the Oglala Sioux Culture Center contains the following:

> The land is a mother who gives not only life and other living things to the Lakota people, but makes them who they are. Without the land, the Lakota people lose their uniqueness. They lose who they have been, who they are, who they can become. The Lakota people have been molded by the land. Without the land, the Lakota people cease to exist.

> To be a Lakota means to be molded by the land. It means in a certain sense, the land claims one.[7]

Smohalla, of the Nez Perce Tribe, spoke concisely and poetically of the same relationship:

> You ask me to plow the ground. Shall I take a knife and tear my mother's breast? Then when I die she will not take me to her bosom to rest.

> You ask me to dig for stone. Shall I dig under her skin for her bones? Then when I die I cannot enter her body to be born again.

> You ask me to cut the grass and make hay and sell it and be rich like white men. But how dare I cut off my mother's hair?[8]

The earth is here described in terms similar to those used to describe the fourth house. Smohalla also states his resistance to placing this fourth-house energy matrix into a context of checks and balances, weighing it against some standard social value (e.g., money), which is the province of Libra and the seventh house. He is clear about what belongs where, and resists misplacement of what he holds sacred.

A second point is the means of the conquest itself. On the Great Plains civilians were hired to kill vast numbers of buffalo, the major source of food, clothing, and tools for the tribes. Thus, the tribes were deprived of their food base and so forced to come to the military forts to prevent starvation. The conquest was not only a military one using firepower from the conqueror's mechanistic and materialistic culture, but also one in which the earth was systematically deprived of its life-giving power. The Plains tribes quickly became a defeated people when their ecological and spiritual base was taken from them.

In astrological terms, the Native Americans were deprived of their connection to those energies symbolized at the nadir. They, therefore, had to redirect their energies to seventh house or Libran matters: treaties and welfare allotments (weighed amounts, checks and balances, negotiations). To them, earth had been "nontransferable real estate"; the idea that land could be bought or sold, or that so much land could be weighed against money (Libra's scales), was unthinkable. The results, in terms of their sense of alienation and loss, are still visible today.

Throughout this process and up to the present day, protection of Mother Earth from the invading and ecologically destructive newcomers has been a deeply emotional issue. Native American rhetoric of the past two centuries expresses a deep horror, not only at the loss of their traditional ways of life, but also at the way the "root of life itself" was jeopardized. This horror is a recurrent theme in their recorded speeches, a theme which comes from all tribes and all geographical areas. And the emotion is related not to intimacy or partnership, but to earth itself, to the center. A few examples will suffice (the interested reader is referred to *Touch the Earth* and *Indian Oratory*).

> The man who sat on the ground in his tipi meditating on life and its meaning, accepting the kinship of all creatures and acknowledging unity with the universe of things was infusing into his being the true essence of civilization. And

when native man left off this form of development, his
humanization was retarded in growth.
Chief Luther Standing Bear[9]
Lakota tribe

A long time ago this land belonged to our fathers; but when
I go up to the river I see camps of soldiers on its banks.
These soldiers cut down my timber; they kill my buffalo;
and when I see that, my heart feels like bursting; I feel
sorry.
Satanta, Kiowa tribe[10]

Frank Waters, contemporary novelist and ethnologist, sums
up the problem:

> ... the white newcomers had committed the one sin against
> which the great spirit, Masaw, had warned the arriving
> Hopis. They had cut themselves off from the roots of life.[11]

A final point is related to the trans-Saturnian planets. It
is that the final stage of conquest was inaugurated by the discovery of gold in California in 1848. The Gold Rush that followed was an example, on a mass scale, of turning the
nontransferable real estate of earth into eminently transferable
currency, which resulted from the "weighing" of gold. Earth
became a commodity. This mass emotionalism closely followed the 1846 discovery of Neptune, the ruler of mass emotionalism, mass movement, and mass delusion. Neptune was
in the sign of Aquarius at the time of its discovery, reiterating
(through the rulership of Uranus) the connection to alienation via the technology that would follow.

The uprootedness illustrated by these historical references
is naturally reflected in the forms which emphasize intimacy
in our culture. The point is not to make value judgments as
to which cultural forms are more or less advanced, but simply to indicate that in Native American societies as in Euro-
pean societies before the rise of industrialism, intimacy and
marriage did not have to supply people with emotion or belonging. This is not to say that there was no emotion in marriage or romantic love, but only to suggest that emotion was
not found only or primarily there; that, from the evidence

of what their spokespeople say, these people had a strong feeling connecting them to the planet that remained the ground of their lives. Lacking such a connection, we must seek the energy in some other level of fourth-house symbolism. This is the subject of the next section.

A Unified World

> He who knows the always—so has room
>   in him for everything.
> He who has room in him for everything
>   is without prejudice.
>
> Tao Te Ching, *Chapter XVI*

Words, diagrams, and an analysis of symbolism can lead us toward a conceptual understanding of the relationship between the living earth, emotion, and the energies of intimate partnership. But how shall these concepts become part of the vital fabric of our lives? How shall we integrate concept with experience? Conceptual understanding is like a road map: it may make a journey possible by making the territory familiar, but it does not necessarily make it easier. A path over a mountain is no easier to walk just because it has been mapped. The journey toward integration is a long and difficult one. It may even be endless; but we must at least begin, knowing that "the journey of a thousand leagues began with what was under the feet."[12]

Carl Jung wrote that psychological problems are not resolved on the same level at which they occur. The hero must find a *new* way to certainty, an approach which goes beyond familiar methods, to discover the true law of his being. This does not mean that we need to be "above it all" to solve the riddles of fulfilling intimacy. It certainly doesn't mean becoming more abstract, or taking a more encompassing but less vital approach.

This new level is an inner, more concrete, vital *and* encompassing understanding of the law of our being in actual manifestation. Our journey is by an inward spiral, not an elevator; in the realm of emotion there is no high or low, only more or less inclusive. The contradictions or polarities of our outer lives may be resolved in the more encompassing "center" described in the preceding pages.

When confronting the sandstorms of the Gobi Desert, G.I. Gurdjieff did not deal with the sand directly. He advocated the use of stilts, noting that the sandstorm did not rise very far above the ground.[13] The use of stilts required a firm sense of rootedness. Similarly, we need rootedness in order to deal with problems in intimacy; but our dealings may not be with the intimacies themselves. According to the logic of the symbolism, our work must involve establishing or reaffirming an emotional tie to earth itself. Seen from this perspective, questions immediately arise: How shall we establish this emotional relationship (fourth house) with an earth that is poisoned, barren, and with which we feel so little connection? How shall we work with the contemporary economic and political situation so as to bring life to earth, or prevent its ecological death? And given such economic strictures and structures as we have, how shall we "go back to the soil"? Where is the soil to go back to? Above all, even if it is possible to "go home again", what good will it do if we carry our inner alienations with us?

Any solution must begin with the situation as it is, and to accept that situation, even if only provisionally, as a working basis. How shall we relate to the present situation in order to find the necessary emotional connections or rootedness that will enable us to create lasting, fulfilling intimacies? This is the question to which our inquiry leads, and if we are to be consistent we should seek the answer in the same symbolism in which the question was framed.

One of the more common symbolic associations of the fourth house is with the mothering principle.* A mother's love for her child is undivided and uncategorical. She may discipline her child's behavior, but she loves the whole child. She re-

---

*Some astrologers would connect the fourth house to the father, not the mother. There seems to be evidence to support either parent's connection to this house, and this is not the place to resolve the issue. In any case, the house may be seen as an area of experience more than a particular parental figure, and is as described above: rootedness, earth-centeredness, and the inner world. This seems to describe the mother more than the father, and the lunar symbols as a whole support this point of view.

lates to the child as a complete being, not as an assortment of traits among which she can pick and choose, accepting those she likes and rejecting those she dislikes. Even if the child has faults—and the mother need not be blind to them—a mother's love is encompassing.

This sort of encompassing love must underlie or imbue all of our intimacies, and must be the basis for our feeling at home on the planet. This is the love that gives the gift of life to all situations, without stint or question. It is the basis of benevolence and of compassion, and we must find it within ourselves, radiating out impartially towards everything and everyone in the world, but doing so from an inner center, symbolized by the Midnight Sun.

This nondualistic love is the basis for social and spiritual development and for any path that unites them. Gampopa, twelfth-century Tibetan Buddhist saint and scholar, recommended the example of a mother's love as the basis for benevolence that forms the heart of the spiritual path, and the love we bear our mother as the basis for active compassion.[14]

In pretechnological times, perhaps it was not so difficult to feel this emotion. The earth was often considered the mother of all creatures. The mother principle was omnipresent and universal, and accorded unquestioned respect. The Earth Mother nurtured all people, and people gave love, respect, and ceremony in return. The earth's rigors were inseparable from its ongoing gift of life: winter gave way to spring, to the full flowering of life which could not take place without winter's period of hibernation and retreat. Whether in man or in nature, the gift of life was cyclic, and hence connected with the female, the mother. Because the whole cycle is necessary, it did not make sense to choose which parts of the mother to accept and which to reject.

Today it does not seem so easy to accept all that we see. The natural cycles of life, though still present, are not as clearly seen. The rigors of our lives have an artificial flavor: on cold mornings our difficulty is not with the cold itself, but with unresponsive steel and sluggish oil in a car that won't start. Beyond that, the world fairly cries out for our value judgments: on all sides we see destruction, useless death, poisoning of the earth, and a system of distribution of resources that is blatantly unfair and cruel.

This may seem far afield from the issue of emotion and intimacy, but we need to cultivate a nonjudgmental acceptance of our world if we are to give birth to fulfilling intimacy. To dichotomize life into what we accept and what we reject is alien to the emotional, encompassing qualities associated with the fourth house, with the love of a mother, and with those energies that emerge in symbolic form from the collective unconscious of the race.

We must accept that the ogres of the world nightmare are part of us, even when they appear as external events. (This issue was discussed from a different angle in the second chapter.) To reject them is to reject parts of ourselves and to block the only sort of progress that will ever really change the world: the progress of deepened, widened, heightened consciousness and awareness. To improve the external situation in the world, we must begin by accepting that world as a mother accepts her child; to improve our intimacies, we must extend the same benevolence to ourselves. The acceptance we must cultivate is the same: the emphasis remains on the inner world. As Jung pointed out, "The upheaval in our world and the upheaval in consciousness is one and the same."[15] We must come home to ourselves with a mothering acceptance, and so give birth to true emotion, the basis of all true intimacy.

This is the path we must travel. But how shall we do so, and how will we know if we stray from it? The answer will not be any one recommended practice or path, because this encompassing acceptance is part of many paths. It does seem that a guide is necessary, lest we pave the way to unhappiness with good intentions: the discovery of Chiron seems to indicate that this need is particularly important now if we are to make the leap from ego's concerns to the insight (Uranus) that can lead to compassion (Neptune) and change (Pluto).

As in the other chapters, the conclusion here is that we must seek a spiritual path, a spiritual solution. The need to reunite our polarized world view is actually a spiritual task. The Buddhist tradition—particularly the peaceful and wrathful deities of *The Tibetan Book of the Dead*—is particularly relevant here. These deities are experienced by the deceased person in the *"bardo"*—the realm to which consciousness goes after death on its journey towards rebirth. The attending lama instructs the dying person to look at these vibrant, emanating deities and recognize that their peaceful or wrathful appearances—and even the deities themselves—are his own projections. The peaceful and wrathful forms are essentially one and the same, and not different from the "Great Light." The dying person is encouraged to:

> . . . recognize whatever visions appear as the reflection of mine own consciousness.
>
> . . .
>
> May I not fear the bands of Peaceful and Wrathful Deities, mine own thought-forms.[16]

It is important to recognize that *The Tibetan Book of the Dead* is applicable to experiences in life as well. Chogyam Trungpa points out in his introduction to the text:

> Bardo means gap; it is not only the interval of suspension after we die but also suspension in the living situation; death happens in the living situation as well. The bardo experience is part of our basic psychological make-up. There are all kinds of bardo experiences happening to us all the time, experiences of paranoia and uncertainty in everyday life; it is like not being sure of our ground, not knowing quite what we have asked for or what we are getting into. So this book is not only a message for those who are going to die and those who are already dead, but it is also a message for those already born; birth and death apply to everybody constantly, at this very moment.[17]

This is directly relevant to our discussion. First, the peaceful and wrathful events of our personal (or political) world may be seen as a dichotomy projected from ourselves, from our own inner division, just as the apparitions are projected from consciousness in the *bardo*. When confronted with a "gap" in our lives, we habitually look into a conceptual framework of good and bad; we fill up the gaps with thinking, with duality in some form. We do not accept experience for what it is, for on one level the gap is an opening that allows us to see clearly. But we resist this.

Partnerships generally result from choice (at least in contemporary society where we choose our partners). Choice results from or rises out of a conceptual framework. The conceptual framework serves to solidify various points of view which separate one from the truth and vital energy of direct experience. It is too often our conceptual frameworks superimposed on our "natural, generalized feeling" which prevent us from seeing clearly or feeling fully, or from "experiencing in the good way of being part of"[18] the root of wisdom symbolized at the nadir.

The horizontal axis of a birthchart symbolizes not so much the dualistic concepts (which are more of a third house-ninth house matter), but the actual dualism of experience that results. This basic dualism is I-other, or separation-judgment (Aries-Libra) in which we make judgments based on our assumption of separation, our sense of ourselves as individual units of action. Dane Rudhyar pointed out that the Libran scales symbolize a weighing process based on a socially accepted standard weight. One such standard weight is ego's conviction of its own potency for action. But a more mature judgment takes place when the sense of separation has gone through the growth process symbolized by the first six signs and houses, particularly that of Cancer and the nadir, where one develops emotional depth and the yearning to be part of something greater and to give the gift of life. The wisdom of judgments that do not include this level of being is questionable.

In any case, our conceptual schemata are never solid. They are full of gaps which offer a glimpse of center, of a common humanity and a unity with others. This experience is often painful because it opens us to the world without the shield of our judgments; to the suffering of birth, old age, sickness, and death. Openness to this basic level of experience is not conceptual but emotional. It closely parallels the symbolism of the nadir and fourth house, which include in their associations the beginning and the end of life.

How shall we contact this center, this empty place where we experience life directly, without conceptual overlays? The preceding material alludes to various spiritual traditions which provide paths to such a center: Buddhism, Taoism, the work of Gurdjieff, and Christianity. What is needed is something to *do*, something practical that begins at the beginning. If we follow this logic again, we get an idea of what "beginning at the beginning" means in this case:

1. We need to reconnect to the center and all it implies according to the symbolism presented here—an empty center.
2. This is no longer possible via the earth itself, but needs to be understood psychologically.
3. This means nonjudgmental love, the love of a mother.
4. Our judgments are based on our conceptual framework, and hence on our thought process.
5. Our thought process is full of gaps that reveal again the empty center.
6. Therefore one may well begin with the thought process and experience there the natural openings, or gaps, that can lead to reconnection. The same may be said for our habitual patterns: seeing them, accepting them, and then seeing through them can give us glimpses of the same openness.

That the thought process leads to the empty center is revealed astrologically by the third house (thinking, duality) leading directly to the nadir, the center, which gives birth to viable relationships: the fourth-house results from working on the third-house experience. On one hand, the third-house experience may prevent us from seeing the center clearly; on the other, working with thought reveals it.

Working backwards farther, to deal with the thought process (third-house), we must develop the qualities of the second house: earthly value, management and practical stability, and groundedness. We must know what is valuable at the level of life-giving potency, the Taurean manifestation of Venusian value (as distinct from the Libran manifestation of value according to a socially accepted standard). Here too is the need to remain firmly grounded and practical in those values. The Buddha exemplifies this Taurean approach because he became immovable once he saw what is valuable: egolessness.

This stability results from proper identification: Aries and the first house. Most people identify with the ego and its physical separation, the spirit identifying with the flesh. But it is possible to identify with the life breath instead of the body to which it gives life: prana, the first and ongoing breath, associated with the ascendant. (Aries is mythologically the ram which was offered to God by people who identified themselves with the offering. Many of us identify with our body, symbolized by the ascendant. The issue is one of proper identification, the enlightened use of the energy of life.)

Hidden here is a description of shamatha (mindfulness) meditation practice: working on the thought process through physical stability (and stability of values) based on proper identification and energy direction; identifying with the universal (Aries-Pisces connection), stabilizing the body (Taurus), and looking at the dualistic mind (Gemini).

It may seem facile to suggest a spiritual solution to an interpersonal issue, but the logic of our inquiry leads to this conclusion. Problems in the collective may be seen as a projection into the environment of energies which are actually potential components of man's spiritual growth. This is consistent with the conclusion of the third chapter. Recalling those projections to ourselves is the best way to work with the problem.

This logic, based on astrological symbolism, might be called a logic of spiritual necessity or spiritual demand. Overall, humankind has reached a point in its evolution where spiritual development has become a pragmatic necessity. Simply put, solutions based on ego are not workable any more than are solutions based on nationalism, ego's political result and reflection. That this need is the primary message for the modern world is indicated by the symbology of the trans-Saturnian planets which tell us that time has run out. The advantage of such astrological symbolism lies in its perennial wisdom; it points us in the right direction while distilling the problem into its basic elements.

In reference to relationship, this means that we must see beyond the idea of two isolated individuals interacting. This demands the development of benevolence, based in the symbolism of love for and by one's mother, which is also a choiceless kind of acceptance of the world and of oneself. Emotion can be poured into and through the world this way, so that not only will partnerships grow from the fertile soil provided, but the world itself, receiving this energy, might become more vibrant.

Acceptance of the world is inseparable from acceptance of oneself. In the Buddhist tradition, one gives rise to *maitri* (kindness to oneself), and this becomes the basis for *karuna* (compassion, kindness, and benevolence toward others). To be kind to ourselves, we must know ourselves. This is not so easy, because of habit. But the symbolism suggests that in the daily round (clockwise direction), habit patterns emerge as thought (fourth house to the third). Understanding our thought patterns is therefore a road to self-acceptance.

Meditation—or the spiritual path—brings about this acceptance. The so-called negative energies are acknowledged and transmuted, a process which can only come about after full acceptance (the mother symbolism) of their energy as it is. This acceptance is applied directly to the thought process (third house) through a stability (second house) infused with energy resulting from identification (first house) with that which is not really separate from the whole (twelfth house). The connection between the twelfth house and the first, or between Pisces and Aries, is related to the sacrifice of the Arian pascal lamb, the sacrifice of separative ego to a higher principle, based on universal vision.

We began by speaking of the instability of relationships in the contemporary world. The logic of astrological symbolism had led to the notion that only the spiritual path will lead us back to that depth of emotion that will give birth to fulfilling relationships. This is true, but we should beware of assuming a simple stability.

The point is that the spiritual path itself can produce instability; to ego it is the ultimate instability, astrologically indicated by the three outer planets. So when we speak of stability in relationship, we need to recognize that if we base our relationship (and relatedness) on our spiritual growth, the relationships which are based in ego and its defenses are doomed to even less stability than before. Any partnership that is based on ego gratification will not survive when the spiritual path overturns ego and uproots its various foundations.

If one is committed to move beyond ego—or beyond its bureaucracy, symbolized by Saturn—then the notion of social function or standardized weight (seventh house, Libra; Saturn's exaltation)* takes on a different look. The standardized weight may be emptiness, non-ego; the social function may be to dissolve ego. This may seem strange, but it is corroborated by Venus's exaltation in Pisces: the love and relational nature is exalted or takes its energy from the universal, from the dissolving of ego. Relationship takes its power from the ability to let go.

Spiritual growth demands this letting go, but we need to distinguish between chaos resulting from letting go, and chaos resulting from ego's holding on. For people on the path, the situations that arise will no doubt be a mix of these. The desire for permanence in relationship is often just ego's desire for security. This type of permanence is actually undermined by the approach suggested here. On the other hand, this approach does seem to offer a deeper sense of relatedness if one is able to give up the desire for ego security. So there is a paradox: enduring, fulfilling relationships can arise best when one gives up the desire to have them. Venus works best when sacrificing self for others (Pisces).

Our fear of separation is not so much due to the separation itself but to there being nothing beyond or beneath it, no fourth-house rootedness in the form of an extended family or ancestral home. Among certain Native American tribes, a marriage could be ended by the wife simply throwing the husband's belongings out of the tepee. The relationship ended, but there remained the tribe or clan, the fourth-house matrix or support for both husband and wife.

On one level, spiritual work may take away some of this support. Yet various spiritual traditions have recognized the importance of developing a wider community of aspirants in which the rootedness of universal acceptance (the nadir of a chart) can be practiced, developed, and extended. Examples

---

*See the glossary for an explanation of exaltation.

of such communities are the Buddhist sangha, the Christian "Mystical Body of Christ," and Gurdjieff's school-groups. When Jesus told his disciples they should love one another, he didn't mean they should have a lot of intimate partnerships. His words apply more to fourth-house symbolism than to seventh.

We might say that our relationship with the world should become like that of a T'ai Chi master: if an adversary attacks, the master simply (and without thought) responds with his T'ai Chi form, the "Great Ultimate." He accepts the incoming energy without hesitation, then neutralizes it, creating energy and harmony through the interplay and reconciliation of opposites, yin and yang. The result is effective action, energy, upliftedness; the ability to work with the energies of the world. The basis of the form in working with yin and yang and not making value judgments is akin to fourth-house energy. Working effectively with the world is analogous to the seventh house.

The fourth house, then, is quite like the Mother of all forms, the Tao. According to Taoist thought, appropriate action is based in nonaction. Nonaction leads us downward, toward the astrological nadir, the center of the earth, which is geologically in a molten state and hence reconciles opposites. This molten state suggests that acceptance is not always easy. Jung wrote:

> At first we cannot see beyond the path that leads downward to dark and hateful things—but not light or beauty will come from the man who cannot bear this sight.[19]

It is a great challenge to reach this level of acceptance, but it is not necessary to achieve complete integration of this type before we can think of fulfilling relationships. The emphasis is on the path, the journey, and the commitment to it. The notion of complete integration is itself dualistic. To accept fourth-house energy does not mean finding a place to stand so that, like Archimedes, we can alter things as we see fit. Integration is a process, not a place. We take part in it by developing a proper, accepting relationship toward ourselves, which is largely a fourth-house matter.

What is required is a commitment to base our intimacies on the deepest roots of our being, on an attitude of motherly acceptance. This is our center, both personally and as a race. We need to recognize our oneness with all creatures, and with the processes of earth itself, to enable ourselves to drop the strategies with which we so often approach the world, ourselves, and our intimacies.

Strategies are associated with enemies, with duality, and are based on an assumption of essential separation. Strategy is also related to the seventh house (of open enemies) and to conquest. Conquering, as many mystics have pointed out, often entails loss of soul. The term "soul" returns us again to fourth-house symbolism: we lose our souls when we try to strategize and conquer, when we get lost in dualism, when we lose our connection to the center and its essential emptiness. When we lose this connection, we lose our souls—or the soul goes out of our partnerships—just as surely as a conquering general sees his troops lose heart from weariness and from being away from home.

Simply put, without fourth-house depth, seventh-house lovers do not hold together. They often become open enemies. Without the motherly love of the nadir, the Venusian love of the seventh house turns into the Furies, who are of the same blood. Intimate relations become conquests; we try to conquer what we really wish to love. But that which is deeply rooted has no thought of conquest, for conquest rises from basic insecurity about who we are.

In all of this, the nadir, the traditional astrological symbol for security, undergoes a curious but important transformation. Instead of a deep, solid sense of identity, it becomes the insecurity of seeing that we have no place to stand, that ego is not solid, even (or especially!) at the root, that the root of our being reaches down into a realm that does away with all the distinctions upon which our security is based. This radical or root insecurity is, paradoxically, the greatest security we can find. So we are left with the curious but reasonable notion that unless we accept our oneness with or belonging to

the whole world—an acceptance which will serve to dissolve
ego—we will not be able to find fulfillment in our intimate
relationships or elsewhere.

Venus is born from a shell that floats on the ocean. This
is not the most secure symbol of love. She is rooted in that
which accepts and gives life to all; and also that which is char-
acterized, underneath, by a life-and-death process in which
all creatures are inextricably tied together. However many
garlands she wears, she is one of the gods, and must be true
to her nature and her generation. If we are to work with her
(seventh house), we must understand her background (nadir).

The Nadir and the Inner Life

The application of the foregoing ideas to individual horoscopes involves paying closer attention to the ruler of the nadir
when looking at the relationship profile and to the nadir itself. In this way, such a profile becomes a more complete picture of a person's individuality.

The nadir is generally a part of interpretation, but usually
it is interpreted as the home or "feeling at home" or the innermost world. This is obviously correct, as far as it goes; but
here the nadir is seen specifically as the root from which relationship grows.

The zodiacal sign on the nadir will be an indicator of the
type of energy through which an individual is most likely to
find that depth of experience, that deep emotionality which
lies at the base of individual growth and consciousness. It can
also indicate the type of habitual pattern which can make true
relatedness and relationship difficult. The sign on the nadir
will indicate one's approach to, or orientation toward, the experience of universality and choiceless acceptance (mother
symbolism) described above. Therefore, though we are speaking of emotion, or "generalized feeling," some people may take
a more practical, or a more speculative, or even active approach to it, depending on the sign at the bottom of their
chart. For example, Capricorn on the nadir indicates emotional depth acquired through discipline, or through some

sense of mission involved with a practical or tangible need. Scorpio on the nadir may indicate that the experience of center will involve intense, emotional encounters where the individual is truly able to lose himself or allow himself to die to his old self-conception. It may also indicate the finding of center through work of a transformative nature. Libra at the nadir may indicate that the center is found through aesthetics or through partnership, cooperation, and social function.

An important point is that the individual approach to the experience of universal, empty center is distinguished from the energy of that center itself. This does not at all invalidate either the individual approach or the basic nature of the energy. Potentially, both can be enriched, though there may be a challenge involved. Libra, for example, may shy away from the emotional depth involved; yet by bringing perspective and balance to it, the depth can be enriched.

Also involved are planets that might be located in the fourth house or at the nadir itself. These will indicate the psychological factors that will be involved most directly in the experience that has been described. Jupiter here may bring one's powers of mental integration (e.g., philosophy, religion) to bear in one's understanding; and lead to realization that the experience of center is important to one's whole sense of general social outreach. Mars in the fourth may indicate that one feels compelled to act directly on the basis of this feeling (I know a number of people with this placement who work directly for the improvement of the environment, the earth as non-transferrable real estate.) The Sun here will indicate that the centering experience is integral to one's entire conscious identity and sense of creativity, though there may be a danger of mistaking the arrogant ego center (Sun) for the universal center which is shared by all. The horoscope of Herman Melville has already been cited as an example of this position. Neptune in the fourth house means that one's need for a mystical or idealized vision is part of one's path to the empty center. In combination with Saturn it seems, first, to require a difficult blending of the ideal and the real, and second, to attune one to those life activities that can combine these two needs, such as the arts or the spiritual life. An example is a woman who had Saturn and Neptune conjunct in Libra in her fourth house, with the Moon added into the conjuction. For many years she ran a dance and theatre studio in her home, often using the space for group meditation as well.

The sign and house position of the nadir's ruler are also significant pointers to where an individual may experience this centering. For example, a woman's horoscope has Aquarius on the nadir, and Uranus conjunct Moon in the eighth house. She works with an innovative psychology program which helps people transform themselves through community involvement. Though this is her career, the implication is that it serves to unite her with the wider human family in a profound way. Another horoscope has Aries on the nadir and Mars in Pisces in the third house, indicating great communicative energy within her immediate environment, connected with an identification (Mars) with either the mystical or the dissolving. This woman is a stimulating conversationalist while socializing after mediation sessions. She also maintains a strong meditation practice, the identification of Mars with those Piscean practices which dissolve ego. She finds her root through identifying herself (Aries, Mars) with egolessness; and part of this identification takes a vivacious, social form, in the interactions resulting from gatherings based on spiritual practice.

In determining the relationship between the experience of center found at the nadir and the needs in relationship found at the descendant, it is important to examine the relationship between the two rulers. This can be done by aspect, by house and sign position and through contemplating the Sabian symbols associated with each planet's degree of longitude.*

In general, the usual rules apply here, except that one adds the notion that the needs of the nadir will find expression through the house and sign position of the nadir's ruler. Stephen Arroyo, contemporary astrologer and author, wrote that one will get information on one's true vocation by considering the house position of the midheaven ruler.[20] The ruler

---

*See the glossary for an explanation of Sabian symbols.

of the nadir indicates, by house position, that life area which leads to the experience of center, which is so essential to true relatedness. The sign position (particularly for the inner planets) indicates the type of energy that is promulgated in this life area; and if the ruler is a trans-Saturnian planet, the person may find centeredness through involvement in some collective or transformative purpose.

The Sabian symbol information is also of great benefit. It can provide nuances of meaning not necessarily present in the usual analysis of the horoscope. The images of these symbols also have a numinous quality not tied to any specific life area, but which, through the hint of a type of response, often contain valuable guidance about the path. The relationship between the symbols of the rulers of the nadir and the descendant will relate these two life areas through the images involved.

The interpretation of the Sabian symbols tends to be subjective, since each individual responds in a different way to the symbolic material. Nevertheless, we sketch an example. If the nadir ruler is in the eighth degree of Sagittarius, the symbol is given as;

> Within the depths of the earth, new elements being formed.[21]

Dane Rudhyar has done a contemporary reinterpretation of the Sabian symbols, giving as the keynote of this system, "The alchemical fire which both purifies and transforms the very substance of man's inner life...PSYCHIC GESTATION."[22] This seems a very appropriate symbol for the nadir, in its relation to the inner life and to new birth (mother symbolism). The emphasis is on a marked inner dynamism; the symbol emphasizes depth and heat and transformation.

If the descendant ruler is in the twelfth degree of Pisces, the symbol reads,

> In the sanctuary of an occult brotherhood, newly initiated members are being examined and their character tested.[23]

Rudhyar notes the keyword as "Qualification."

This may also seem an appropriate symbol for the descendant, indicating as it does a form of weighing or testing. In connection to the previous symbol, though the aspect between the two rulers is a square,* there seems to be common ground in these two symbols, which both contain such strong hints of transformation and spiritual growth.

A slightly different picture is presented if the descendant's ruler is found in the eighth degree of Pisces:

> A girl blowing a bugle.[24]

Rudhyar's keynote here is, "A call to participation in the service of the race, as an evolutionary crisis approaches."[25]

Here it seems that the centering, transformative process indicated by the "psychic gestation" symbol associated with the nadir is called upon to develop, through partnership, some sense of wider participation. The relationship between nadir and descendant, in terms of their rulers, seems to be one of mission, of service, and certainly connects to something beyond the restrictions of narrow egohood.

This interpretation is obviously incomplete, involving only the Sabian symbols and leaving out the information of houses, signs, and planets. Nevertheless, it should give some rudimentary idea about how the material in this chapter is connected to actual interpretation; but it may tend to be an interpretation rooted in a sense of universality. This is as it should be.

---

*See the glossary under Aspects for an explanation of a square.

8

The Illusory Prison:
Astrology, Freedom, and Ego

Only he that rids himself forever of desire
can see the Secret Essences;
He that has never rid himself of desire can
see only the outcomes.
Tao Te Ching, *Chapter I*

Astrology, God, and Ego

The question of whether or not we have free will has permeated
the stream of Western philosophical thought. In religion, many
have pondered whether the presence of an omnipotent and
omniscient God implies a negation of our freedom of choice
or will. In politics and law, the individual's right to exercise
freedom of choice has been polarized to the requirements of
"an orderly society," which in turn is often believed to make
"higher achievements" possible (or at least to facilitate them).
Psychoanalysts have suggested that we are in thrall to our own
blind urges and instinctual drives.

The term "freedom" carries a different meaning in each of
the above allusions. Nevertheless, the lack of freedom in each

143

case implies a situation in which "I"—or one's self-conception—is circumscribed, impeded, or possibly even negated. In a culture like our own in which individualism is held in such great and unquestioned esteem, the limitation of ego's latitude has almost always been considered negative. We can therefore expect considerable resistance to any system of thought, such as astrology, that has called this latitude into question or suggested that it might be merely illusory.

It is notable that the fear of astrological accuracy, especially in the art of prediction (which generally refers to what astrologers term "transits"), has many parallels to the fears and logical difficulties surrounding the idea of an omniscient and omnipotent God. In both cases, the ability to see into the future seems to imply that freedom of choice is severely limited, if not totally nonexistent. In both cases, too, the uninformed observer tends to assume the existence of coercive, external forces which overpower or logically negate the strength or reality of the human will. In both cases, it is generally assumed that there is an active, causative agent (the deity, or in astrology the heavenly bodies) and something acted upon (humanity).

Many will resist astrological insights because of this imagined fatalism, even though astrological interpretations do not assume and are not based on the existence of external, celestial, compelling forces. Similarly, there are many who resist the idea of God because of a fear of losing freedom, even though St. John's Gospel clearly states that "the Kingdom of God is within you."

This parallel between astrology and religion is not surprising. In ancient times, the two were strongly linked, and the courtship has continued into the modern era, even though the relationship has become somewhat more stormy and uneven than in former times. At times, the study of astrological symbolism was said to reveal the workings of God to mankind; at others, the same symbols were rejected outright because they were seen as vehicles of human pride in its attempt to understand the workings of the deity. P. I. H. Naylor writes in his *Astrology: a Fascinating History:*

> Officially, the Church rallied to Augustine, condemned the subject of astrology as impious. In practice, its supporters

and great men did a remarkable amount of talking and writing about astrological ideas. The attempt to define free will and, at the same time, to acknowledge a Divine Plan inevitably brought astrological philosophy right into the picture.[1]

The difference between astrology and traditional religion shown here is that religion attempts to reconcile the will of God with man's free will, while astrology demonstrates the nature of the relationship between that human will and celestial events.

At times, of course, astrological indications have been taken as synonymous with the will of God; but as belief in God has become much less firm, the question of freedom has been directed more and more toward the "effect" of the supposed "celestial forces." This is significant in two major ways. First, whether or not we can say that God exists, the planets are plainly observable; their existence is verified by the senses or technological extensions thereof. The question often becomes: If the stars and planets make us what we are and cause us to do what we do, how can we claim that we are free? This replaces the older question: If the Will of God makes us what we are and is the prime mover of the universe, how can we say that we are free?

The second thing to realize in this discussion is that as our notions about God become less and less firm, there may be a parallel process in our notions of ego, however unconscious this change may be. Our concepts about God parallel our concepts about ego, at least in the popular mind: a solid ego holds together one's personal universe; a solid God, functioning in an egolike way, holds together the cosmos.

Astrology in the West has been developed in cultures that do not, by and large, question the validity of ego. Yet, as the first half of this book attempts to demonstrate, the astrological symbols themselves depict not only of the process of growth and attempted crystallization of ego, but also of its transformation. Further, the very fact that the astrological symbols relate human experience to a frame of reference (the heavenly bodies) which is in constant movement, suggests that the notion of solid, unchanging entities, such as egos, is illusory. Therefore, since astrology calls our notions of ego severely into question, and since it is ego that wishes to be free, it behooves us to examine the implications of astrological symbolism for the idea of freedom.

Clearing Away Faulty Assumptions

The first step in such an examination is to clear away faulty assumptions. One of the major of these is contained in the above question about the stars and planets making us what we are. This assumes a mechanistic world view in which certain solid bodies affect other solid bodies, and in which this is the only explanation for connections between entities. In other words, the notion that the stars and planets "make us what we are" implies that there is a causal relationship existing between heavenly bodies and human behavior or consciousness. The view is understandable when we consider that the planets were once considered to be gods with definite, wilful influences on human life. It is further understandable in light of the Newtonian, mechanistic view that still dominates modern consciousness, despite increased evidence as to its insufficiency.

The fact is, however, that modern astrology is not based on such an assumption or such a mechanistic model. The point is not that such a causal relationship is impossible, but that, on the one hand it is not a necessary condition for accurate astrological work, and on the other hand, it is not verifiable. Most importantly, mechanistic causality is not the only model for meaningful, trustworthy connections between events. In his *Principles of Astrology*, C.E.O. Carter, noted English astrologer, wrote:

> It would be premature, at this stage, and in a work of this nature, to discuss whether the heavenly bodies affect us directly as causative agents, or whether there is simply a correspondence between their motions and positions and the natures and destinies of human races and individuals.[2]

Further on, he adds that the "bodies of the solar system indicate, if they do not produce" the situations one observes; his definition of astrology is that it is "the science of certain cryptic relations between the celestial bodies and terrestrial life."

Astrological work is based on the fact that there is an observable, trustworthy, and meaningful connection between the macrocosm (heavenly bodies) and the microcosm (man). It does not necessarily comment upon the nature of that connection, but stresses that: 1) the ongoing changes in that connection can be delineated accurately through the use of appropriate astrological methodology; and 2) the connection is not only related to external events but to internal events, meaning, and even wisdom.

As such, the relationship between macrocosm and microcosm seems much more synchronistic than causal. The term "synchronicity" was coined by C. G. Jung. In his book of the same title, he calls synchronicity "an acausal connecting principle" and explains it as follows:

> I chose this term because the simultaneous occurence of two meaningfully but not causally connected events seemed to me an essential criterion. I am therefore using the general concept of synchronicity in the special sense of a coincidence in time of two or more causally unrelated events which have the same or similar meaning.[3]

Thus the meaning of events or life periods can be described on a number of different levels; but the fact that describing this meaning in terms of the symbolism of a particular planet in transit related to a planet in the natal chart does not imply that the connection is causal.

As noted before, the assumption of causality is quite understandable when we consider the history of Western scientific and philosophical thought. Until recently, Western science has seen the universe in cause-and-effect terms: It's prime symbol has been Newton's falling apple; its symbolic force has been gravity, based on solid bodies affecting each other in a measurable but not meaningful way. In this view, measurable and impersonal forces grind out a mechanical universe, and solid entities (as egos imagine themselves to be) become part of the mechanics. In this world view there is cause to fear for our freedom.

Though astrology is not usually associated with quantum mechanics, the two have at least one similarity in that they provide clear evidence that causal forces do not by any means account for all the possible connections between entities. Astrology further demonstrates that what we call distinct entities, such as planets and humans, may not be as separate as we have believed, or may not be separate in the same way. Thus astrology runs counter to much of traditional Western science, dissolving its supports, providing new insights, giving a more universal view, and finally providing an avenue through which people may completely transform their view of the universe in which they live.

Astrologers will notice a parallel in this threefold process of change to the threefold process of ego-transformation described through the symbolism of Uranus, Neptune, and Pluto (Chapter Five). Science, like ego, will resist change; and like ego it will be forced to change through its own inner logic, which is the result of what it discovers. The resistance to astrological insight may be seen, therefore, to reflect the more basic resistance of ego itself, here using science to preserve its sense of potency and integrity through clinging to those abstract concepts that seem to give it support.

Astrological practice in general, and transit study in particular, serve to undermine ego's security at this level through presenting an altogether different world view, thus undermining ego through undermining its conceptual support. On a crude level, this may occur through allowing people to see that their assumptions about time (i.e., that one cannot know the future) need to be reconsidered. On a subtler level, people are called upon to revise their whole relationship to the phenomenal world, as they begin to see how what happens "out there" is not really separate from what happens "in here." That is, the planets are not really separate, or not as facilely separate, from experience as we have tended to believe; nor is our experience of the phenomenal world so different from our "inner psychological dynamic." These two revisions are both implied by accepting guidance from astrological transit study. As a result of undermining the sense of "I," these alternate views also undermine the sense of freedom, because it is generally the "I," or ego, that wishes to be free.

In order to become more precise in this discussion, we need a more precise understanding of the term "freedom" itself. What do we mean when we say we are free or have freedom of choice? "Freedom" is one of those all-encompassing words that is understood in different ways. It is necessary to narrow the focus.

In this discussion, freedom will be considered initially from two perspectives: First, there is freedom *from* certain forces, people, or coercions, and there is freedom *for* certain activities, expressions, or states of being. A man in prison is likely to be concerned primarily with the first sort of freedom. He wishes to be free from the confinement in which he is placed; and though he may have in mind certain activities or projects he will be free *for* once he is out of prison, freedom *from* his confinement is his initial concern. On the other hand, the creative artist is primarily concerned with freedom *for* creative endeavor: the freedom to create, or the ability to do so. Though the artist may wish to be free *from* various constrictions, such as the necessity to work eight hours a day to support himself, his primary focus will remain on his freedom *for* creation.

The two categories may interpenetrate. A prisoner may have creative aspirations and an artist may become preoccupied with obstacles to his creative endeavors. Nonetheless, though not absolute, the twofold distinction is useful as a starting point for discussion.

When people see astrological symbolism as a threat to free will, they are generally viewing freedom in the first sense: the celestial bodies are seen as potentially coercive forces from which one would like to be free. In such a case, astrological symbolism is seen as indicating outside forces which, being potent, threaten ego's cherished latitude and attitude. So two related issues are raised: 1) that of the externality of the energies involved, and 2) the whole issue of coercion. The latter is actually an issue of form. There is no question that the plane-

tary movements are correlated to human experience in a trustworthy way, and this correlation implies that human
experience has a form and rhythm that can be delineated. The
question is whether we see this form as an indication of
constriction or of potential empowerment.

The issue of externality is closely related to that of causality, but its resolution is more subtle. Transits will often seem
to be external events. For one thing, they are related to phenomenal events, planetary movements, and usually manifest
through experience in the phenomenal world of tangible experience. Transits are not usually only states of mind without
clear external referents (as might be expected with progressions). Many astrologers, however, will interpret a transit as
an "event" with both internal and external manifestations, seeing internal and external worlds as reflections of each other.
In this view, those who feel that they are imprisoned or coerced
by celestial forces are really being held back or tested by their
own inner energies.

The notion that the internal world and the external world
are an inseparable continuum is not really new. The teachings of Hinduism and Buddhism both present the idea, though
in different ways. The following Zen koan from the *Mumonkan*
(1228 A.D.) puts the issue into clear focus and even suggests the
primacy of mind over the events of the external world:

> The wind was flapping a temple flag. Two monks were
> arguing about it. One said the flag was moving; the other
> said the wind was moving. Arguing back and forth, they
> could come to no agreement. The Sixth Patriarch said, "It
> is neither the wind nor the flag that is moving. It is your
> mind that is moving." The two monks were struck with
> awe.[4]

Another example of this view comes from the American
Southwest, where certain native tribes believe that the rising
of the sun depends on their continued prayers and ceremon-
ies. This belief and practice expresses a viewpoint congruent
with the astrological notion that the sun is not only a celestial
body but also an internal energy, dependent on human faith
for its full manifestation.

Traditional astrological methodology indicates the unity of the internal and the external by assigning each sign to a certain organ or part of the human body. This is a specific use of the general principle, "as above, so below," which lies at the base of astrological thinking. The planets and the zodiac are seen as within the body as well as outside. Accurate results yielded by this system of correspondences indicate that the notion of man as a microcosm of the universe is not only a metaphor but a principle of praxis.

The point to be made from this unity is that if transit study seems to threaten a person's feeling of freedom, the real threat comes from within, not from coercive forces "out there," but from a rhythm and demand which is intimately related to the most natural growth and development of each person. Growth demands certain limitations and is actually inseparable from the limitations or conditions that make it possible. A plant grows only under certain conditions; it is not "free" to depart from those conditions and still live. A deeper freedom is found within the conditions needed for growth itself, and this freedom is *in* the growth, more properly related to the potentials that arise from growth than to the conditions which make it possible. As noted above, form may be empowering.

This is as true on the level of spiritual development as it is on the level of physical growth. Spiritual growth, which may also be seen as growth in increased freedom from psychological strictures which define ego, requires some binding. This is the principle behind vows and voluntary disciplines in various religions or groups which seek to bring about this growth. So form, far from being coercive, may be seen as the ground of our spiritual or creative growth. Problems arise when form becomes an end in itself. Nevertheless, it remains true that while ego will wish, in order to maintain its illusory conviction of potency, to be free *from* limitations, the creative spirit will wish to be free *for* the demands of its own development and unfoldment. It turns out that, in order to be free *for* creative work, it is necessary to be free *from* the restrictions of ego, or to engage in such a freeing process. Ego is the prison house we all wish to be free from, and the bars of the prison are not so much the formal requirements indicated by transits (or the natal chart), but ego's attitude toward them.

The Empowering Nature of Form

The term "freedom for" implies some degree of potency for action, and it is important to be precise in what is meant. What does it mean to be able to *do* something? Could this ability to do be illusory? P.D. Ouspensky writes in *The Fourth Way:*

> One of the most important and most difficult illusions to conquer is our conviction that we can *do*. Try to understand what that means. We think that we make a plan, decide, start, and achieve what we want, but the system explains that man 1, 2, and 3—men dominated respectively by the instinctual, emotional, and intellectual functions—cannot 'do', cannot do anything, everything just happens to him. That may sound strange, particularly now when everybody thinks they can do something. But little by little you will understand that many things we are accustomed to say about man generally could only be true of men of higher level and do not apply to men of our low level.[5]

Ouspensky's words are reminiscent of the Buddhist notion that men are driven by the "winds of karma," which is motivation and motivatedness. Motivation manifests as thinking; one of the thoughts is that one is a free agent. One object of Buddhist training is to see the emptiness, fickleness, and delusive nature of the thought process itself. From an astrological perspective, karma is depicted in the birthchart as a basic allotment, and through transits and progressions in the way that allotment works out in time and environment. The implications of both Buddhism and astrology seem to be that, though one has no choice about the allotment itself, having "made one's bed," there *is* choice about how to work with it. The same could be said for the rhythm which that allotment expresses through time.

Astrology can help us to see that our motivation is mechanical. The study of transits does this most graphically, as I will describe later. But the entire ordering of the astrological symbols (as described in Chapters Two through Four) shows that human experience itself develops according to certain archetypal patterns, irrespective of the individual. The planets do this in psychological terms, the houses in terms of the logic of personal outreach, and the signs in terms of basic patterns of energy. These archetypal patterns in other systems, such as the Buddhist *skandhas* and *nidanas,* have many parallels to the planets and signs respectively. Also, transitting planets move from one sign to another, depicting the karmic pattern on a collective level. Individuals participate in this pattern through its interworking with the patterns of the birthchart.

Astrological information can empower us on one level by giving us an understanding of such patterns: We see how the world works, what its rhythm is, so that, understanding, we can participate more fully. Such information can further empower us by giving us a conceptual knife to cut through many of our cherished illusions regarding ego. Since one of these is that we are free, we may find it threatening; but by definition creativity steps beyond the status quo, psychological or social, and is therefore threatening on some level by its very nature. Astrology can in this way open us to a wider perspective, one not dependent on ego and its various blinding and constricting demands. If we follow the astrological indications faithfully, which means to stop resisting the natural development of our experience, we may begin to develop to Ouspensky's "higher level" where true "doing" becomes possible. To accomplish this means to bind ourselves to certain limitations.

How does a person stop resisting the predictable but natural rhythm of his experience and of life in general? Two major forms of resistance will likely be: the attempt to escape pain, and the continuing effort to establish one's potency. In astrological terms, the first seems to be a resistance to the information about individual transits, such as Saturn or the trans-Saturnian planets challenging personal planets or angles. Paradoxically, ego's resistance to the growth-demands indicated by such transits serves to increase the pain, not decrease it, for the growth demands going beyond ego. Ego increases its own pain by holding to its crystallizations (Saturn).

The second form of resistance to life's rhythms—the continuing effort to establish one's potency—is usually a more general resistance to the whole idea of being circumscribed. Some transits will bring this more sharply into focus than others. For example, Saturn squaring the Sun or Mars will focus the issue more pointedly than would a trine from transitting Jupiter to the same natal planets. But the predictability associated with either transit brings up the same larger issue of how much one is able to actualize experience "on one's own."

Because of these two types of resistance, any discussion of freedom must include an understanding of the nature of and need for suffering, and of the empowering nature of form. In regard to the first, a study of transits can give a person a sense of meaning within or rising from one's pain. Such an analysis can give perspective and objectivity, give the ability to understand one's present situation from the standpoint of one's entire life or of one's habitual, karmic patterns. The developmental purpose of suffering can be made clear, that major, challenging transits demand change at a deep level. Understanding the meaning of a transit can make one's response conscious and therefore more likely to lead to real change.

In regard to the empowering nature of form, a person can see that an insistence on seeing pattern as merely limiting is itself merely a point of view, not a true assessment of the situation. Perceiving limitations as only negative blinds us to our potentials. For example, humans have no wings with their particular skeletal structure (ruled by Saturn, the planet of limitation), but this lack of wings does not mean that we can't fly. Early attempts to fool nature by attaching mechanical wings to one's arms did not get us very far. In fact, we would probably have never become airborne if we had simply complained about lack of freedom in respect to flying. We learned to fly by accepting limitations.

The indications of natal charts and the transits to them may be viewed in a similar way. If we ignore them, we become like a man flapping his attached wings, not coming to terms with limitation. Properly handled, however, the information of transits, combined with one's willingness to accept them as the formal fabric of one's life, can lead one to true flight, or to the actualization of one's true potential as a human being.

This means that we need to suspend our judgments about our experience and not be always trying to decide what is best for us, what we need, or even what we want. Jesus at Gethsemane, asked the Father, a Saturnian figure, if the cup of his crucifixion might pass from him. Perhaps the Father either could not or would not relent; as symbolized by Saturn, his purpose could have been to narrow the focus of experience, forcing Jesus to look carefully and closely at something. As the symbol of the reaping of karma, Saturn could not alter the decree of what must be reaped. Jesus submitted to the Father's will (Saturn), and through his developed insight (Uranus) could see that the needs of the world demanded his compassion and sacrifice (Neptune), his death, and rebirth into power (Pluto).

The point here is that transformational power comes through experience if we are able to suspend judgment and to develop equanimity in the face of difficulty. This is not a stoic equanimity but the equanimity of Neptune, in which one's vision is sufficiently encompassing to accept all possibilities. This sort of choicelessness seems to be an extremely important goal and turning point in our modern situation, as symbolized by Neptune's position as the outermost planet at this time (until the year 1999—Chapter Five).

The empowering nature of form is central to the arts, and stands out quite clearly there. The sonnet, for example, may at first seem an arbitrary form: line length, meter, and rhyme all must follow a specified pattern. New students of poetry and writing may see this as a barrier, but it is safe to say that the great sonneteers saw this form as a potential, as a positive medium for poetry, an ideal vehicle through which to release meaning. Many of the great English poets used the sonnet form, which may indicate that those writers were drawn to its strict demands to give power to what they wished to say. In some mysterious way, the strictness of form brings forth sublimity. Poetic energy is empowered by the form through which it emerges.

Sonneteers are rare these days. Poets write in idiosyncratic forms; and yet, as Robert Frost wrote, no verse is really free verse. Communication, poetic or otherwise, must partake of form; even if the form has no name or is strictly individual and unique to a particular work, there must be some sort of order. Language itself is formal: without form it would be a series of meaningless verbal gestures.

The form or patterns of life represented by astrological symbolism are analogous to the form of a poem, for astrology is itself a language. The delineation of a chart by the astrologer is akin to the *explication du texte* which brings out or explains the meanings of that poem. The explication does not *cause* the poem to have meaning; nor does it limit the meanings that a poem expresses. A poem certainly doesn't become meaningful simply because a critic writes about it, any more than a person becomes meaningful or follows a certain life pattern simply because he or she has seen an astrologer. Nonetheless, just as one puts some faith in the way a sensitive literary critic illuminates a poem (perhaps because his insights accord with one's experience, or bring to conscious awareness what may have been merely "felt"), so one can put faith in the reliable reading of a natal chart. The primacy of the poem, or individual experience, is not threatened.

Nor does the form of human life—both generic and individual—threaten the full experience of living. Seeing the form can enable one to make that experience even richer. In this, too, astrology is like poetry: it not only enables one to see the richness already present, but through its insight further enriches one's life through expanded awareness and sensitivity.

If one were to ask But why the form at all?, the reply might be simply that it's impossible to have it otherwise. The question assumes that form and life are distinct, an assumption by no means borne out by experience. As Zen Master Shunryu Suzuki noted in connection with Japanese painting, even the attempt to be formless ends up having form:

> Ancient painters used to practice painting dots on paper in artistic disorder. This is rather difficult. Even though you try to do it, usually what you do is arranged in some order. You think you can control it, but you cannot; it is

almost impossible to arrange your dots out of order. It is the same with taking care of your everyday life.[6]

We could say that astrological symbolism shows patterns of human growth, and that even if we attempt to escape these patterns, we end up by falling into them. As noted before, we become subject to what we try to escape from.

Empowerment through Submission to Transits

In order to focus this discussion, I can give a few examples. The first is the event described by transitting Saturn conjuncting the natal Sun, certainly a transit which is likely to make one feel less free in the conventional sense. Its symbolism indicates a restriction (Saturn) of creative vitality (Sun) and its limitation due to the way one has structured one's world. Saturn limits and focuses experience so that a person structures his world too narrowly. Eventually circumstances and developmental need force him to pay attention to his basic sense of vitality and creative radiation. Poor health and low energy are not uncommon at this time; they are another manifestation of the general sense of restriction.

So here the particular limitations of the transit itself (that is, its own limiting nature) are added to any sense of limitation resulting from expectation of constriction at the time of the transit. Such a period can become very constrictive indeed if one fights against its demands and fails to recognize its potential. Saturn is particularly difficult in this regard, often manifesting as a trickster with deceptive joyfulness.

The potentials of the time are in learning how to organize and focus our energy, or learning on a very tangible level how our fears inhibit creativity. We can make great strides by working directly with those fears, thereby making them part of the durability and groundedness of our creativity. We can learn about the tangible sources of our vitality and creativity—perhaps its structural component in the body—and learn to put that vitality forth in more enduring forms or structural ways, making it not only more honest, but also more practical.

Those who see this transit as a restriction from which they

would like to be free are likely merely to feel thwarted. Such people will miss the great opportunity to concentrate their vitality and consolidate their efforts, the opportunity to see the ways in which they've wasted their vitality in the past. Because the transit is usually a fairly difficult one, people may be blinded by their suffering, and so resist it. But it is fruitless to wish that the transit—the period of transition—will go away or not happen at all. If one's sense of freedom is no more than the wish to be free from difficulty, a Saturn transit will never seem freeing. If, however, one's wish to be free includes the willingness to accept and work with suffering as part of one's path, then the period of the transit will be an opportunity.

Another example, of quite a different nature, is when Uranus is transitting in square aspect to natal Mars. Uranus symbolizes rapid change, born from new insight or ideas, and a strong desire to break free of old restrictions; intuition percolates through one's world. Uranus acts particularly on self-assertiveness (Mars), the way one initiates things, and on the physical body or desire nature. Uranus speeds up the rhythm of life and can be very wilful in the changes it causes. These changes are often perceived as necessary, either because of one's notion of truth, based on fixed ideas or new insights, or a need to express one's "individual genius."

This transit, therefore, indicates sudden self-assertion and anger and perhaps inappropriate self-expression leading to disputes. One may try too hard, feel extremely wilful, and have trouble communicating, because the highly charged energy of one's ideas is not in harmony with the way one reaches out. What is required is a way to create life-structures, either psychological or in the world (depending on whether the aspect is the waning square or the waxing one*) through which one can discover new methods of self-assertion. These should be more in line with one's own ideas and notion of truth and possibly with new currents in collective thought as well.

---

*See the glossary under "Aspects" for an explanation of waxing and waning aspects.

The uneven energy of this transit may result in accidents if one doesn't find, or refuses to seek, new avenues of self-assertion. In such a case, the accident shakes one up sufficiently to cause one to change. The message emerges from the environment.

The conceptual knowledge of this transit can lead to some empowering. One may not feel free to relax and to be passive. At such a time passivity does not seem the most productive course and may even be destructive, forcing the disruptive energy to come *at* us (as in an accident). Thus one loses the ability to consciously bring about change. The transit's limitation is the need to alter one's habitual way of asserting oneself. Its empowerment is that now, through disruptions that arise from one's own percolating intuition, there is great opportunity to do precisely that.

The last example is the transit of Neptune opposite (180 degree aspect) one's natal Venus. The negative feeling of limitation here is a period of illusions and disillusionment in how one relates to others, especially at an intimate level. One may become involved in relationships based on the partner's dissipation or helplessness or based on overidealization in some form.

The opposition from Neptune indicates the need to incorporate, through objective awareness, this idealism and selflessness (the positive manifestation of dissipation) into one's life, particularly through one's intimate encounters or affections. One needs to live from a more selfless perspective. Venus indicates relationship, how one expresses affection, and the issue of valuation. The opposition reiterates the importance of relationship as the mode of growth with this transit. One needs to come to a more objective awareness of how affectional needs and idealism need to interact, and for partners to see each other more objectively. This need for objectivity is markedly different from the energy of Neptune, making this a particularly problematic transit for relationship.

One becomes limited if content to, or insistent upon, living with unquestioned idealism. One becomes free by distinguishing such things as martyrdom from selflessness, idealistic dream worlds from true spirituality. The opposition demands objectivity. Venus is artistic technique, Neptune inspiration; so the freeing potential may be an objective awareness of the relation between the two. One can bring artistic inspiration to one's aesthetic sensibilities or to one's intimacies. One can either have a truly universalized perspective on relationship, or a perspective that is simply unfocused, preferring an ideal with little relation to things as they are.

In each of these examples, astrological symbols bring forth meanings that might otherwise remain hidden in events, and in such a way that energy can find a way to express most positively. The negative expressions are generally those which refuse to recognize the needs of the time, preferring something else, and which therefore miss the opportunities presented. In the words of the quotation that begins this chapter, such expressions are based on desire, and therefore miss the "Secret Essences."

These symbols present the true needs and demands of the time, giving "that glimpse of truth for which you have forgotten to ask;"[7] and it is this truth, and our willingness to act according to it, which will set us free. We become free by submitting ourselves to a process of growth, and to the binding factors inherent in it, both in chaos and in peace. In terms of the natal chart, this process of growth goes naturally beyond ego, and the demand is that one submit to the process of transformation. Submission is, paradoxically, to take active part. In terms of transits, the process of growth is in cooperation with the pattern of available energy.

Freedom and Ego

We all base our notions of freedom on the desires of the ego. We have seen, so far, how concern about the implications of astrology on our freedom is mostly misguided fear of coercion arising from external "forces." At the same time, one may wish to be free *for* certain activities; but this wish may not only be another desire of ego, but in itself quite mechanical and predictable. The problem is that ego wants something in the first place: either freedom from coercion or the ability to establish itself in its own potency.

So, in speaking about freedom, we need to be clear that it is ego that wants to be free. This is actually a contradiction, because as we have seen, the process of ego itself is one of restriction. Ego itself is a prison and remains so no matter how big the jail cell seems to be.

Furthermore, ego and its notions of freedom refer back and forth to each other as mutually dependent, seesawing reference points. Ego wishes to be free and creates its own definitions and views of freedom, which continually refer back to ego itself. This need for reference point—for "me" and something to confirm "me"—makes true freedom impossible.

True freedom must be free of the restrictions contained in ego. The logic is straightforward and worth summarizing:

1. The desire for freedom is ego's desire.
2. Ego itself is an imprisonment based on just such desires. (In the Buddhist tradition, "ego" is defined through the continual circle of desire, hatred, and stupidity. Desire is linked to attachment, including the often-unconscious attachment to one's sense of "I.")[8]
3. Therefore, any real freedom must be free of ego. Any process of freeing must involve becoming free of the limitations and ignorance of ego. This process begins by seeing the pattern of egoic imprisonment clearly. This clarity then becomes the working basis for the transformational path.
4. Therefore the only way to find true freedom is through walking the spiritual path, which means a path which sees through the illusion of ego. To walk this path requires some discipline, some limitation, and a recognition of the inescapability of suffering.
5. Ego will naturally resist this process because this sort of freedom requires not only that it must limit its cherished illusion of latitude, but also that it must die. Ego's resistance, in part, takes the form of thought and concept, through which it convinces itself that it can be and is free; or that everything is okay.

As discussed before (Chapters Two, Three, and Four) ego attempts to maintain itself on a moment-to-moment basis by keeping itself entertained with its thoughts, creating an opaque world. Meditation works backwards through this process. In astrological symbolism, meditation is grounded in Saturn, the final symbol of ego's limitation and of limitation or discipline generally. So we can say that growth toward freedom begins by facing and working with our limitations and our resulting sense of insecurity and doubt. The issue then becomes not so much whether or not we are free, but how we will work toward freedom. Saturnian discipline on the spiritual path is based on conceptual knowledge or a wider view (Jupiter) which has sufficient perspective to see the pattern of limitation. The ability to focus energy (Mars) is also involved. These three planets together comprise the energy of outreach (since they are outside the orbit of Earth). They can lead ego to recognize the first flash of freedom (Uranus) for what it is—the insight that illuminates the realm beyond ego, or gives the first intimation that such a realm exists. Saturnian discipline, or adherence to form, gives the ability to see this vision, or take in this insight, without losing one's sense of presence.

As noted above, another support for ego is its imagined volition. Study of astrological transits (and, perhaps less obviously, of other techniques of time analysis) demonstrates the choiceless nature and mechanical manifestation of this volition. If the natal chart shows the nature of what we will seek in life, and the transits may be said to show the rhythm or schedule of the search, where is the choice? The astrological symbols shows us the parameters through which our volition will work.

This is not a simple matter; there is no single symbol to which one can point as indicating volition. Volition is symbolized by the complex interweavings of the entire chart. For example, the volition of a person with a T-square involving Pluto will be quite different from the volition of someone with a T-square involving Neptune.* And even these indications will be much

*See glossary for an explanation of T-square.

modified by other horoscopic factors. (If the T-square involving Pluto shows a trine to Jupiter from Pluto, this indicates that the transformational imperative of Pluto will be much aided by expanded, abstract perspective, or perhaps by the study of philosophy, literature, or religion. On the other hand, if the trine from Pluto is to Venus in the seventh house, volition toward transformation will likely involve affectional relationships with others.)

From the paradigm of volition symbolized in the natal chart, transits (and other methods of time analysis) take on a deeper meaning, showing how volition manifests mechanically through time, and then how this manifestation always relates back to basic patterns of attachment. At the same time, transits can provide guidelines on how to move beyond those patterns of attachment toward what we might call the potentiality for liberation presenting itself through experience.

Since our seeming volition is actually mechanical, the choices, desires, and hopes upon which ego bases so many of its assumptions of potency actually indicate its bondage. A study of this mechanicalness can bring an insight that it is not really possible for ego to be free. Furthermore, the illusion of freedom is made more convincing by ego's cherished assumptions about its latitude and potency. Ego cannot be free because it is itself a prison. The only path to true freedom is through an increase of consciousness; but this requires an honest look at things as they are. Ouspensky wrote:

> Attaining consciousness is connected with the gradual liberation from mechanicalness, for man as he is is fully and completely under mechanical laws. The more a man attains consciousness, the more he leaves mechanicalness, which means he becomes more free from accidental mechanical laws.[9]

And later:

> As long as he does not realize that he is simply a machine and that all his processes are mechanical, he cannot begin to study himself, for this realization is the beginning of self-study.[10]

Astrology can be of assistance here by providing a more ob-

jective perspective on our mechanicalness, on our patterns of
clinging and volition, and on our lack of control over the basic
patterning of our experience. (This is *not* the same as saying
we are fated to experience particular events.)

As noted above, the path beyond mechanicalness, or beyond
ego, seems to include submission, discipline, energy, concept
and acceptance of the choicelessness of situations. The astrological symbolism demonstrates why we need to submit, what
sort of ongoing energy we submit to, and the meaning of any
particular submission in the context of our overall development.

In Step with the Dance

We are carried forward by forces and energies which are
much larger than ourselves, yet which are mysteriously inseparable from us. A good deal of anxiety comes from the conviction that we can and must *do* things, that we must act, or even
create the energy of our lives all by ourselves. This assumption
may be more prevalent in the West than in the East, but it
seems to be one of the more difficult byproducts of the indi-
vidualized state of consciousness. The problematic futility of
such an attitude is evident in the *Tao Te Ching*, which speaks
of the power which emerges from precisely the opposite point
of view, the approach of the Sage:

> Is it not just because he does not strive
>   for any personal end
> That all his personal ends are fulfilled?[11]

It is somewhat relaxing, and probably a seed of wisdom, to
realize that we are not as important as we would like to insist.
Energy is not only something we create by ourselves but a
pattern in which we participate. Growth in awareness comes
not so much from the ability to create energy outside of this
pattern, but rather to participate more completely in what is
already present. Astrology can help us to understand the ongoing pattern of this energy, first in its archetypal form, and
then in its relation to personal patterns of attachment. Through
this developing understanding, we can come to greater partic-

ipation, which is greater freedom in the sense of fuller output
of energy. This can only result from not worrying about freedom, not insisting that one must have it.

In the Buddhist tradition, there is an analogous concept to
that of ongoing patterns of energy. With this "self-existing
energy," the emphasis is again on participation. Chogyam
Trungpa explains this from the point of view of tantric
Buddhism:

> Self-existing energy is not dependent on something or
> somebody else; it simply takes place continuously. Although
> the source of such energy is difficult to track down, it is
> universal and all-pervasive. It happens by itself, naturally.
> It is based on enthusiasm as well as freedom: enthusiasm
> in the sense that we trust what we are doing, and freedom
> in the sense that we are completely certain that we are not
> going to be imprisoned by our own energy, but instead,
> freed constantly. In other words, we realize that such
> energy does come up by itself, and that we can work with
> it. This self-existing energy is the potentiality of *siddhi*, a
> Sanskrit word that refers to the ability to use the existing
> energies of the universe in a very special and appropriate
> way.[12]

Trungpa refers to this energy as "basically . . . the energy of
the psychological realm," and goes on to point out that it is
valid and powerful in a way that goes beyond our concepts
of good or bad:

> This energy is created both when we fail to do something
> and when we accomplish something. Rejection or accep-
> tance by the world does not mean that the energy is either
> invalid or valid. Rather, there is transparent energy hap-
> pening all the time. Whether we are in an appropriate sit-
> uation, in accordance with the laws of the universe, or we
> are in an inappropriate situation, not in accordance with
> the laws of the universe, energy is constantly taking place.
> This energy, from the vajrayana or tantric point of view,
> is simply the energy that exists.[13]

Participating in this energy is somewhat like taking part in
a vast, orderly dance. Perhaps it is a waltz, which, though it
is never exactly the same at any two moments and may seem
full of mad whirling about, is nevertheless composed of clear,

repeating patterns which can be seen by the discerning eye. In order to take part properly, one must let oneself go with the ongoing rhythm while at the same time remaining aware of one's coordination with other dancers, with the ongoing music, and with the space itself. This coordination may include various technical aspects of waltzing, but one needn't be discouraged if one doesn't know all the particulars. For one thing, it's important to listen to the music, to "get a feel for it," rather than worrying about what one doesn't know. Beyond that, it is largely one's *attitude* that creates harmony, not the particular dance steps; and one's attitude needs to be willingness to drop, as much as possible, the ongoing emphasis on one's own importance. The analogous statement in astrology is that it's less important to know the technical meanings of the transits, than to be able to sense and trust the ongoing pattern of one's life, and to loosen one's self-insistence.

In waltzing, as in life, thinking egocentrically is usually counterproductive. If one holds back—due to thinking about oneself, or even how well one is doing—the rhythm is lost. Holding back also inhibits one's awareness of others, so that one does not sense the ongoing rhythm of the phenomenal world. The result is likely to be collisions, losses of rhythm, and possibly consequent discouragement, leading to further collisions as one gets caught in the chain reaction of ego, which is suffering. The problem is not so much that one gets out of rhythm—for there are many astrological transits which tend to put one out of rhythm with the rest of the world in an extreme way—but that one refers back constantly to ego, to judgment, to reference points.

Letting go to the larger rhythm does not mean absolving oneself of responsiblity. Still less does it mean losing precision. To let go means to let go of a self-reference point, the sense of a solid, centralized "I" that prevents full precision and responsibility. This means letting go of the insistence on a solidified center, and accepting that any center is simply the power of "the space where there is nothing, that the usefulness of the wheel depends."[14]

This logic is taking us closer to a conception of freedom that is not based on external events. Astrologically, the pattern of

these events is apparently unalterable: the blueprint or schedule of one's life is laid down at birth, and an astrologer may
plot out all patterns of transit and progression (or other time
analysis techniques) from the moment of birth. Similarly, when
one enters a waltz, the waltz pattern is what it is; it doesn't
make sense to fox-trot or argue.

Freedom is better approached through attention. We are free
to be attentive, in the dance as in life; and to be fully attentive
is to let go of our central reference point. When we are attentive, we see that it is not external events or patterns that define
freedom, but how we work with what is presented. It is a question of wakefulness, not of predictability. Freedom is within
and made possible by attention (which includes attention to
our imprisonment).

It is important to note that this attention does not promise
harmony; but part of the attention is to notice the disharmony,
not only in any present situation, but also in relation to our
patterns of attachment (or paradigm of volition). To do this
requires a sense of humor, which is in itself a detachment from
ego's central control. We might then see that stumbling along
out of step might be in rhythm with some wider or less visible
dance, just as a Chaplin-like figure in a movie might be out
of rhythm with visible events but in perfect rhythm with the
sound track, which is presumably not heard in the environment
of the film, but which creates a wider harmony. This cultivation of humor is particularly necessary during the challenging
transits of Saturn and Pluto: the cultivation of not taking ourselves too seriously, of letting go, is on some level the meaning
of the transits themselves.

The larger harmony may be beyond the scope of our awareness, just as the sound track of a movie is presumably beyond
the awareness of the stumbling Chaplin figure. This points to
our need to develop sensitivity to the world, so that we are able
to sense the subtleties of energy that compose it. Our perspective
can be that just as dissonances can create a harmony, so many
out-of-step movements may actually become in step with the
dance.

Also, we need to see how discontent and suffering are part
of a larger pattern, and that anguish is not to be rejected. To

some, harmony may require anguish; they need to cultivate
an attitude toward experience that is aesthetic and nonjudgmental, for the aesthetic perspective sees life in terms of vi-
brancy and depth, not merely good and bad. In other words,
we need to have faith in the patterns of our lives on all levels.
These patterns are the continual weaving of wholeness, and
the wholeness includes our anguish and discontent as well as
our joy in harmonious participation. Astrology can help us to
see how our discontent and suffering *are* part of this larger
wholeness. The natal chart does this in terms of basic patterns;
transits show the developing, or transitional quality of this
wholeness.

Crossing Niagara on a Tight Rope

The acceptance of astrology and the symbolism of astrological transits is simply a matter of being honest and clear about
our experience and trying to learn from it. Like many other
learning processes, this one may begin on a conceptual level,
but slowly we can bring it closer to home, taking to heart what
we learn, and seeing the wisdom.

As this acceptance deepens, internal events may begin to take
precedence over external ones. In T'ai Chi it is said that the
great masters can "do their form" (practice their movements)
completely on an internal level. Deepened acceptance of the
patterns of a dance make it less an exercise and more a reward
for the spirit. All of this recalls Trungpa's words (quoted above)
about self-existing energy being "the energy of the psychological realm." It also recalls the words of Carl Jung:

> We are a psychic process which we do not control, and only
> partly direct...In the end, the only events in my life worth
> telling are those when the imperishable world erupted into
> this transitory one....I can understand myself only in light
> of inner happenings. It is these that have made up the sing-
> ularity of my life.[15]

From an astrological perspective, which has parallels in both
Buddhist and Jungian thought, external events mirror and co-

incide with the need for inner growth. The internal realm cannot really be separated from the external. In his *Planets in Transit*, Robert Hand points out that what we usually call events may be seen as "projections, through which your inner energies are experienced at various different levels of life."[16] Carl Jung spoke of the same connection on a collective level by saying that the upheaval in consciousness and the upheaval in our world are one and the same. At times, too, external events may indicate our refusal to accept the difficulties involved in our personal growth (an issue discussed at length in the fifth chapter).

The process of this inner growth leads us away from ego's fixation on itself as separate from the phenomenal world, but we must accept the intimate messages about the progress of that growth that come from that phenomenal world. Transit study gives us valuable information about the stages or critical points in this process. It will seem to indicate restrictions only to those whose sense of freedom depends on a solid "I" performing "I-generated" events, or to those who resist their own growth and experience.

In the end freedom is demanded from us. This is because true freedom is freedom from the solid centrality of ego, which we must all eventually overcome. The search for freedom, inseparable from freedom itself, is a discipline. It is much like the freedom of a man walking a tightrope spanning Niagara Falls. He is free, in some sense, to step off the rope; but that "freedom" is simply to choose death or, symbolically, the swirling, unconscious maelstrom of the world. His real freedom in his progress toward the other shore is to pay attention to his steps, to learn the freeing discipline of such attention and the balance it brings, and finally, the way such attentiveness enables him to travel to his goal on the other shore.

Astrological transits can help us keep this balance by showing us the nature, power, and timing of those natural events which are likely to become part of our journey, events which induce us to lose attention and balance and increase the danger of our being blown off.

Eventually, we might learn to dance on the rope, to exult with the wind in our mouths, and to realize that though the form of our dance is defined by the rope and the winds, there is still something indefinable in our exultation, and in the suffering it includes.

The world has often been referred to as a prison house. Astrology may at first seem threatening because it demonstrates the structure of the prison, thus bringing our fears to the surface. But in the end it can actually show us the inner structure of the prison house, thus allowing us to escape. It can also show us that the walls of the prison are not solid but permeable, no more solid than the person they surround. In this way, astrological knowledge can be liberating.

Imprisonment began when we were young. We have almost forgotten a time without it, and it is difficult to imagine life without bars. Within our cells we may try to convince ourselves that we have free choice. We can look at the western wall or at the eastern wall or at the ceiling. We feel free to read various books, to order lunch, to stand on our heads, to keep ourselves amused. There seem to be many choices, and we refuse to recognize that even these are mechanical. This is tolerable so long as we remain unaware of the world beyond the prison. But when we see the world outside, life in the cell no longer seems free or tolerable. We retain our guaranteed meals, clothing, protection from the elements, basic necessities; but as soon as we observe the spaciousness outside, we are reminded of the limitation of all of our prison activities. If someone tells us that even in that spacious external world there is some ordering and limitation, we still will wish to go.

But for many years we may not feel free to escape. We believe that we are locked within impervious bars and walls. We are so convinced of the impossibility of escape that we have never given serious thought to attempting it. We may even have convinced ourselves that our glimpses of the spacious world outside were only hallucinations or dreams.

We do not remember—or we choose to forget—that long ago we sat in that vast, open space. Then an old man approached us, calling himself "the Lord of this World," and told us he had something to teach us. He hung walls of paper

around us, gave us drawing materials, and said we could draw
on the paper walls whatever we desired.

So we drew. At first, being familiar with the original vastness, we drew it as best we could, showing distant horizons
with passes going through to the distant hills. Later, becoming unsure and forgetful, we began to draw animals instead,
wild beasts to hold our attention, to give our landscapes
immediacy and excitement. The beasts looked fierce, so we
drew steel bars to keep them out. Finally, to ensure our safety,
we drew a lock for the steel door we put in. We hid the key
so that we might not, in a moment of what we called weakness,
decide to venture out. Eventually, we forgot where we had
hidden the key as well.

Then we sat down in our room. We soon forgot about the
old man and his lessons. We sat surrounded by the objects of
our desires, and we felt content. The old man had promised
us something if we would draw, but we eventually forgot what
it was to be. Seen in this way, all we received was the gift of
our own imprisonment, the walls of our fears.

Astrology can demonstrate the illusory nature of all that we
created for ourselves.

Notes

Chapter 2

1. Frank Waters, *Mountain Dialogues* (Athens, Ohio: Ohio University Press, 1981), 109.

2. Ibid., 111.

3. Alexandra David-Neel, *The Secret Oral Teachings in Tibetan Buddhist Sects* (San Francisco: City Lights Books, 1967), 19.

4. Chogyam Trungpa, *The Myth of Freedom* (Berkeley: Shambhala, 1976), 12.

5. *Tao Te Ching*, Chapter XI.

6. Paul Reps, compiler, *Zen Flesh, Zen Bones* (New York: Doubleday, no date), 31.

7. Idries Shah, *The Way of the Sufi* (New York: E.P. Dutton, 1970), 213.

8. Alan Oken, *Complete Astrology* (New York: Bantam, 1980), 184.

9. *The I Ching or Book of Changes*, translated by Richard Wilhelm and Cary F. Baynes, Bollingen Series XIX (Princeton: Princeton University Press, 1950), 288.

10. *Lankavatara Sutra*. See Lama Anagarika Govinda, *Foundations of Tibetan Mysticism* (New York: Samuel Weiser, 1977), 77-80.

11. Erminie Lantero, *The Continuing Discovery of Chiron* (York Beach, ME: Samuel Weiser, 1983), 17-32.

12. Gampopa, *The Jewel Ornament of Liberation*, translated and annotated by Herbert V. Guenther (Boulder: Prajna Press, 1981), 31.

13. David Neel, *Secret Oral Teachings*, 8.

14. Gampopa, *Jewel Ornament*, 2.

15. Ibid, 30.

16. P.D. Ouspensky, *The Fourth Way* (New York: Vantage Books, 1971), 292.

Chapter 3

1. Dane Rudhyar, *Astrological Signs: The Pulse of Life* (Boulder, CO: Shambhala, 1978), 15.

173

2. Alice A. Bailey, *Esoteric Astrology* (New York: Lucis Publishing, 1951), 92.

3. Rudhyar, *Astrological Signs*, 90.

4. Dane Rudhyar, *The Astrology of Personality* (New York: Doubleday, 1970), 223.

Chapter 4

1. Dane Rudhyar, *The Astrological Houses* (Garden City, New York: Doubleday, 1972), 36ff. Note: This reference is for the term "fields" but not necessarily for the use to which I have put it.

2. Alexander Ruperti, *Cycles of Becoming* (Reno: C.R.C.S. Publications, 1978), 20.

3. Dane Rudhyar, *Form in Astrological Space and Time* (Lakemont, Georgia: C.S.A. Press, 1970), 19.

4. Robert Hand, *Horoscope Symbols* (Rockport, Massachusetts: Para Research, 1981), 264-6.

5. Dane Rudhyar, *The Lunation Cycle* (Berkeley: Shambhala, 1971), 33.

6. Rudhyar, *The Astrological Houses*, 53.

7. Hand, *Horoscope Symbols*, 306.

8. Ibid., 304.

9. W.Y. Evans-Wentz, *The Tibetan Book of the Great Liberation* (New York: Oxford University Press, 1954), 37.

Chapter 5

1. James C. Coleman, James N. Butcher, and Robert C. Carson, *Abnormal Psychology and Modern Life* (Glenview, IL: Scott, Forsman & Co., 1980), glossary.

2. C.G. Jung, *Aion*, Bollingen Series XX, Translated by R.F.C. Hull, (Princeton: Princeton University Press, 1959), 8-35.

3. Liz Greene, *Relating* (York Beach, ME: Samuel Weiser, 1978), 11.

4. Greene, *The Outer Planets*, 14.

5. Chogyam Trungpa, *Cutting Through Spiritual Materialism* (Boulder: Shambhala, 1981), 31ff.

6. Greene, *The Outer Planets*.

7. Rick Fields, *When the Swans Came to the Lake* (Boulder: Shambhala, 1981), 31ff.

8. Ibid., heading material.

9. Chogyam Trungpa, *Meditation in Action* (Berkeley: Shambhala, 1969), 23.

10. Chogyam Trungpa, "Acknowledging Death as the Common Ground of Healing," *Naropa Institute Journal of Psychology*, (Boulder: Nalanda Press), vol 3 (1985), 3.

11. Lantero, *The Continuing Discovery of Chiron.*

12. Liz Greene, *The Astrology of Fate* (York Beach, ME: Samuel Weiser, 1984), 214.

13. Dane Rudhyar, *The Galactic Dimensions of Astrology* (New York: ASI Publishers, 1975), 120.

Chapter 6

1. John Welwood, "Why Are Long-Term Relationships So Difficult Today?" *The Vajradhatu Sun*, October/November 1985 (Boulder: Vajradhatu, 1985), 8.

2. James Joyce, *Ulysses* (New York: Modern Library, 1914).

3. *Webster's New Twentieth Century Dictionary*, Vol I (U.S.A.: William Collins and World, 1975), 594.

4. Hand, *Horoscope Symbols*, 59.

5. Hesoid, *Theogony*, translated by Normal O. Brown (Indianapolis: Bobbs-Merrill, 1953), 58.

6. Matthew 22:14

7. Dane Rudhyar, *The Astrological Houses*, 74.

8. *The I Ching*, 249.

9. Ibid., 714.

10. Ibid., 249.

11. Ibid., 249.

12. Rudhyar, *Astrological Houses*, 74.

13. Hand, *Horoscope Symbols*, 277.

14. Ibid., 278.

15. Lama Anagarika Govinda, *Foundations of Tibetan Mysticism*, 160-62.

16. Ibid., 161-62.

17. P.D. Ouspensky, *The Fourth Way* (New York: Vantage, 1971), 119.

18. Ibid., 403.

19. Marc Edmund Jones, *Astrology: How and Why It Works* (Boulder, CO: Shambhala, 1977), 32-93.

20. Soyen Shaku, *Sermons of a Buddhist Abbot* (New York: Samuel Weiser, 1971), 19.

21. Govinda, *Foundations of Tibetan Mysticism*, 152.

22. Arthur Waley, *The Way and Its Power: A Study of the Tao Te Ching and Its Place in Chinese Thought* (New York: Grove Press, 1958), 149.

Chapter 7

1. Thomas Carlyle, *Critical and Miscellaneous Essays* (New York: D. Appleton and Co., 1867), 188.

2. Rudhyar, *The Astrological Houses*, 95.

3. Carlyle, *Critical and Miscellaneous Essays*, 188.

4. Ibid., 188.

5. *Norton Anthology of English Literature*, Vol. II. (New York: W.W. Norton, 1962), 99.

6. Matthew Arnold, "Dover Beach," in *The Portable Matthew Arnold*, edited by Lionel Trilling (New York: Viking Press, 1949), 149. Copyright 1949 by The Viking Press, Inc., renewed (c) 1976 by Diane Trilling and James Trilling. Reprinted by permission of Viking Penguin, Inc.

7. *Makoce: Curriculum Materials Resource Unit*, Project IH-004 (Pine Ridge, S.D.: Oglala Sioux Cultural Center, Red Cloud Indian School, n.d.), 1.

8. T.C. McLuhan, editor, *Touch the Earth: A Self-Portrait of Indian Existence* (New York: Outerbridge and Dienstfrey, 1971), 56.

9. Ibid., 99.

10. W.C. Vanderwerth, compiler, *Indian Oratory: A Collection of Famous Speeches by Noted Indian Chieftains* (New York: Ballantine Books, 1971), 148.

11. Frank Waters, *Pumpkin Seed Point: Being Within the Hopi* (Chicago: Swallow Press, 1969), 69-70.

12. Waley, *The Way and Its Power*, 221.

13. G.I. Gurdjieff, *Meetings with Remarkable Men* (New York: E.P. Dutton, 1974), 164-76.

14. Gampopa, *The Jewel Ornament of Liberation*, 92ff.

15. Carl Jung, *Modern Man in Search of a Soul* (New York: Harcourt Brace Jovanovitch, 1933), 209, 211.

16. W.Y. Wenz, editor, *The Tibetan Book of the Dead*, Lama Kazi Dawa Samdup, translator (New York: Oxford University Press, 1960), 103.

17. Chogyam Trungpa, translator, *The Tibetan Book of the Dead* (Boulder: Shambhala, 1975), 1-2.

18. John Fire Lame Deer, *Lame Deer Seeker of Visions* (New York: Pocket Books, 1976), 108.

19. Jung, *Modern Man in Search of a Soul*, 215.

20. Stephen Arroyo, *Astrology, Karma, and Transformation* (Vancouver, WA: C.R.C.S. 1978), 223.

21. Dane Rudhyar, *An Astrological Mandala* (New York: Vantage, 1974), 214.

22. Ibid., 214.

23. Ibid., 275.

24. Ibid., 273.

25. Ibid., 273.

Chapter 8

1. P.I.H. Nayler, *Astrology: A Fascinating History* (Hollywood: Wilshire Book Company, 1967), 55.

2. Charles E.O. Carter, *The Principles of Astrology* (Wheaton, IL: Theosophical Publishing House, 1963), 14.

3. Carl Jung, *Synchronicity: An Acausal Connecting Principle, Collected Works,* Bollingen Series XX, Translated by R.F.C. Hull, (Princeton: Princeton University Press, 1973), 25.

4. Zenkei Shibayama, *Zen Comments on the Mumonkan* (New York: Harper & Row, 1974), 209.

5. P.D. Ouspensky, *The Fourth Way,* 18.

6. Shunryu Suzuki, *Zen Mind, Beginner's Mind* (New York: Weatherhill, 1970), 32.

7. Joseph Conrad, "The Nigger of the Narcissus," in *Typhoon and Other Tales* (New York: New American Library, 1983), 21.

8. Osel Tendzin, "The Wheel of Life," *Naropa Institute Journal of Psychology,* Vol I, Number 1 (Boulder: Nalanda Press, 1980), 50-51.

9. Ouspensky, *The Fourth Way,* 29.

10. Ibid., 105.

11. Waley, *The Way and Its Power,* 150.

12. Chogyam Trungpa, *Journey Without Goal: The Tantric Wisdom of the Buddha* (Boulder: Prajna, 1981), 39.

13. Ibid., 40.

14. Waley, *The Way and Its Power,* 155.

15. Carl Jung, *Memories, Dreams, Reflections* (New York: Random House, 1965), 4.

16. Robert Hand, *Planets in Transit* (Rockport, MA: Para-Research, 1976), 6.

Glossary

ASCENDANT In the horoscope, the ascendant is that point in the east, on the horizon, where the sun, moon, and planets rise once each day due to the rotation of the earth. On the circle which outlines the horoscope, there are four points which have special names: the ascendant, the descendant, the midheaven, and the nadir. The midheaven is sometimes referred to as the M.C. or the medium coeli, the nadir as the I.C. or imum coeli. The ascendant is usually shown at the 9 o'clock position on the circle, the descendant at the 3 o'clock location. The midheaven is always at the top of the horoscope and the nadir halfway around at the bottom.

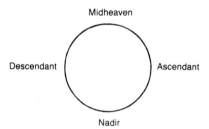

The Sun is at the ascendant at sunrise and at the descendant at sunset. During the morning hours, it "rises" toward the midheaven—that is, the houses revolve over the Sun, which moves through them. The Sun therefore rises into the twelfth house, and if a person is born just after sunrise, it will be posited there. If he is born near noon, the Sun will be at the top of the chart, near the midheaven; if born at sunset, the Sun will be at the descendant; and if near midnight, it will be near the nadir. Planets which are above the horizon (the ascendant-descendant axis) are potentially visible, though of course if the Sun is also there, it will dominate all planets except the Moon (which is considered a planet in astrology).

179

ASPECT. Astrologers judge the effects of one planet acting on another by the aspect between them, which is their angular separation, measured in degrees and minutes of longitude. The most commonly used are the opposition (180 degrees), the square (90 degrees), and the trine (120 degrees). The trine has traditionally been considered benefic, and the other two malefic, though such a division is being modified in contemporary astrology. Squares and oppositions, while usually difficult, symbolize an inner tension or conflict which demands a creative response, while the trine, in producing harmony, can indicate the danger of lassitude. A combination of "hard" aspects (e.g., square, opposition) with "soft" aspects (e.g., trine and sextile, which are 60 degrees) is often considered helpful.

The conjunction (0 degrees) is classified as an aspect only in Western astrology. Its influence can be either harmonious or challenging. Other aspects which are often used are the quincunx (150 degrees, sometimes called the inconjunct), the semi-square (45 degrees), the semi-sextile (30 degrees), the sesquiquadrate (135 degrees), the septile (51 degrees, 25 minutes, formed by dividing the circle by 7), and the quintile (72 degrees, produced by dividing the circle by 5).

Aspects are formed through the various "phases" of interplanetary cycles as seen from the earth. The most evident of these is the soli-lunar cycle, which we experience as the phases of the Moon. Here, as with most other interplanetary relationships, the Sun and Moon go through various key points in their interplanetary cycle: first the conjunction (new moon), then the waxing square (waxing quarter), then the opposition (full Moon), then the waning square (waning quarter, last quarter). This outline gives only the cardinal points; there are also a waxing sextile and a waxing trine, a waning sextile and a waning trine, and so forth.

Astrologically, the waxing aspects are considered differently from the waning aspects: the former are generally associated with spontaneous or exteriorizing activity, the latter with more reflective energy and the "building" of consciousness. For a more complete treatment of the subject, the reader is referred to Dane Rudhyar's *The Lunation Cycle* (Boulder: Shambhala, 1971) and his pamphlet "Form in Astrological Space and Time" (Lakemont, Georgia: C.S.A. Press, 1970).

A T-square is formed when one planet (or more than one if conjunct) forms two square (90 degrees) aspects to the planets which are in opposition (180 degrees) on both ends of an axis, which is 90 degrees to the longitude of the forming planet. In the horoscope, the configuration has the shape of the letter T, the horizonal bar of the T comprising the opposition axis and vertical bar containing the planet forming the squares. The T-square is an indication of a dynamic tension in the psychology of an individual. It can manifest positively as a powerful creative imperative or negatively as inner tension and dissipation of energy.

CUSP OR CUSPAL AREA. In a horoscope a cusp is the demarcation boundary between two signs or houses. Astrologers often extend the notion of cusp from a single line of demarcation to a wider area in which the energy changes from that of one symbol (sign or house) to another. Though there is no definite agreement among astrologers on the precise size of this cuspal area, it is generally felt that it extends from three to seven degrees to one side or to both sides of the actual house cusp, and somewhat less for signs.

DETRIMENT. A planet is astrologically in detriment when it is in the sign opposite (180 degrees from) the one it rules. Also called the position of "dishonor," the detriment position is considered one where the planet (or psychological energy) has difficulty in manifesting harmoniously. Traditionally, this has been considered unfortunate, weakening, or negative, depending on other factors in the chart. While the traditional explanation has much merit, it also seems to be true that the detriment position of a planet is a challenge to look more deeply into the planetary energy involved. Because that energy is blocked in some way, there is an impetus to look at it more deeply or to understand it differently.

ELEMENTS. The signs of the zodiac are classified into the four elements of antiquity: fire (Aries, Leo, Sagittarius), earth (Taurus, Virgo, Capricorn), air (Gemini, Libra, Aquarius), and water (Cancer, Scorpio, Pisces). The ninth house, for example, may hold any sign of any element on its cusp, or leading edge, but it is still regarded symbolically to be of the nature of the ninth sign, which is Sagittarius. Hence, there is a fiery quality to whatever sign and corresponding element is found on the cusp of that particular house, and to whatever planets inhabit it.

EQUIDISTANCE. Equidistance refers to an equal house chart, which we might call the archetypal form of the chart, which will vary according to individual circumstances.

EXALTATION. Exaltations are part of a planetary rulership scheme whereby the planets are deemed to have potency and congeniality in certain signs.

HOROSCOPE. A horoscope or birthchart is a map of the sky taken, like a snapshot, at the moment of an event or birth. It consists of twelve divisions or houses, displayed as a circle with twelve sectors, like the wedges of an orange with twelve sections. The first six houses are always drawn below the horizon, and houses seven through twelve are the wedges above the horizon.

In these houses are placed the various planets according to their longitude, or angular distance from the great circle which contains the vernal equinoctal point, called the First Point of Aries.

Behind the planets is the band of stars through which the Sun and Moon appear to travel across the sky. This band is called the zodiac. It, too, is broken into twelve sectors, in each of which is a collection of stars called a constellation. These twelve particular constellations—out of a total of eighty-eight in the heavens—correspond symbolically with the twelve familiar signs of the zodiac. It is these signs which are of interest to astrologers and which form the backdrop in the stage behind the actors—the planets—in the celestial drama which plays out the constant changes and movements of experience.

It should be noted, however, that the astrological signs of tropical astrology are not the same as astronomical signs. The vernal equinoctal point of one degree Aries, according to the measurements of tropical astrologers, is actually in the early degrees of Pisces. This backward movement of the Aries point is known as the "precession of the equinoxes," and measures the transition of the great astrological ages, such as the present Age of Pisces and the impending Age of Aquarius, which begins when the vernal equinoctal point precesses back into the constellation of Aquarius.

HOUSES. *See* Horoscope.

INNER PLANETS. The inner planets are Mercury, Venus, Mars, Jupiter, and Saturn, and include the Sun and Moon. It is the convention among most astrologers to classify the Sun and Moon as planets when discussing them along with the planets, as one family of astrological influences. However, inner planets often refer only to those within the oribit of the earth: Mercury and Venus.

MIDHEAVEN. *See* Ascendant.

NADIR. *See* Ascendant.

OPPOSITION. *See* Aspects.

PROGRESSION. Astrologers "progress" a horoscope to a certain year after birth by studying how the planets have moved in the same number of days or hours or minutes (depending on the system of progression) after the birth event. Transits, which are different from progressions, are the positions of the planets, Sun, and Moon on any particular day the astrologer might be interested in. For further details on the methods of transits and progressions, the reader is referred to any standard text on astrology, such as *How to Cast a Nativity* by Alan Leo, *Astrology: How and Why it Works* by Marc Edmund Jones, *The Principles of Astrology* by Charles Carter, or *The Practice of Astrology* by Dane Rudhyar.

RULERSHIP. According to a concept handed down from ancient astrologers, each planet is said to "rule" over a certain sign or signs. This means that a planet operates strongly and in greatest accord with its basic nature when it occupies the sign of its rulership. Planetary aspects will modify this strength a great deal, as a planet in its own sign—called its position of dignity or honor—may receive important aspects that strongly challenge the strength of its position.

Before the discovery of Uranus, Neptune, and Pluto, each planet was considered to rule two signs, its "day" sign and its "night" sign. The two "lights," the Sun and Moon, ruled one sign each. With the discovery of new planets, the old rulerships are often still retained, so that with the addition of a rulership for each new planet, there are now some signs with dual rulership. The traditional system of rulerships is given on page 68. The contemporary system with only new rulerships is given on page 69; the system with dual rulerships is as follows:

Aries: Mars	Libra: Venus
Taurus: Venus	Scorpio: Pluto and Mars
Gemini: Mercury	Sagittarius: Jupiter
Cancer: Moon	Capricorn: Saturn
Leo: Sun	Aquarius: Uranus and Saturn
Virgo: Mercury	Pisces: Neptune and Jupiter

Some astrologers would add Pluto as co-ruler of Aries; others would drop some or all of the dual rulerships.

SABIAN SYMBOLS. A Sabian symbol is a line description, key phrase, or key word ascribed to each of the 360 degrees of the zodiacal circle. There are several of these sets of symbols available to astrologers. They add another dimension to the delineations already in the astrologer's traditional portfolio, and are independent of the meanings assigned to the planets and signs and houses in a horoscope. For further information on these symbols, the reader is referred to *An Astrological Mandala* by Dane Rudhyar and *The Sabian Symbols in Astrology* by Marc Edmund Jones.

SIGNS. *See* Horoscope.

SQUARE. *See* Aspects.

TRANSITS. *See* Progression.

TRANSPLUTO. Transpluto as a physical body does not exist or has not been found. It is an imaginary planet used by a small number of astrologers, mainly those of the German school of cosmobiology, which is a form of mathematical astrology. There is an ephemeris for Transpluto which gives its position in the signs, but it is not based on physical observations.

T-SQUARE. *See* Aspects.

WANING. *See* Aspects.

WAXING. *See* Aspects.

ZODIAC. *See* Horoscope.

Index